Microsoft Excel 2013 Advanced

Michelle N. Halsey

ISBN-10: 1-64004-041-2
ISBN-13: 978-1-64004-041-0

Contents

Chapter 1 – Getting Started

Excel is the world's premier spreadsheet software. You can use Excel to analyze numbers, keep track of data, and graphically represent your information. Excel also makes your job easier by providing an easy to use interface, and an array of powerful tools to help you turn your data into useable information – and better information leads to better decision making! At the end of this tutorial, you should be able to:

- Use SmartArt and other objects in worksheets

- Trace precedent cells and dependent cells, as well as use other auditing tools

- Create and work with charts

- Create Pivot Tables and Pivot Charts

- Record and run macros

- Solve formula errors

- Use What If Analysis tools

- Use tools to manage rows, columns, duplicates, and validation

- Group and outline data

Chapter 2 – Smart Art and Objects

SmartArt, pictures, text boxes, and shapes are different ways to enhance your spreadsheet, especially when sharing the information with others. In this chapter, we will look at how to add these objects to your spreadsheets. We will also look at how to edit a SmartArt diagram. Finally, you will learn about the contextual Tools tabs that appear in Excel 2013 when you are working with different types of objects.

Inserting SmartArt

To insert SmartArt, use the following procedure.

Step 1: Select the **Insert** tab from the Ribbon.

Step 2: Select **SmartArt**.

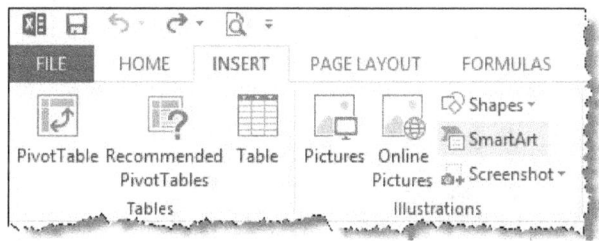

Step 3: In the Choose a SmartArt Graphic dialog box, select the category on the left. Then you select the item in the middle. The right shows a preview of the item. Select **OK** to insert the content.

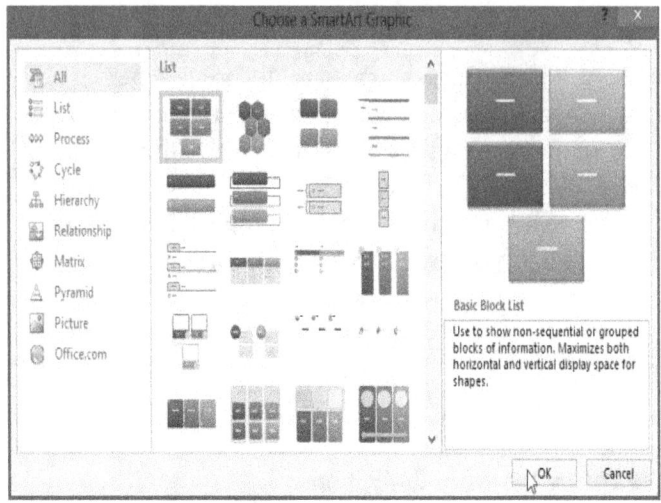

Excel inserts the selected SmartArt graphic in the middle of the spreadsheet.

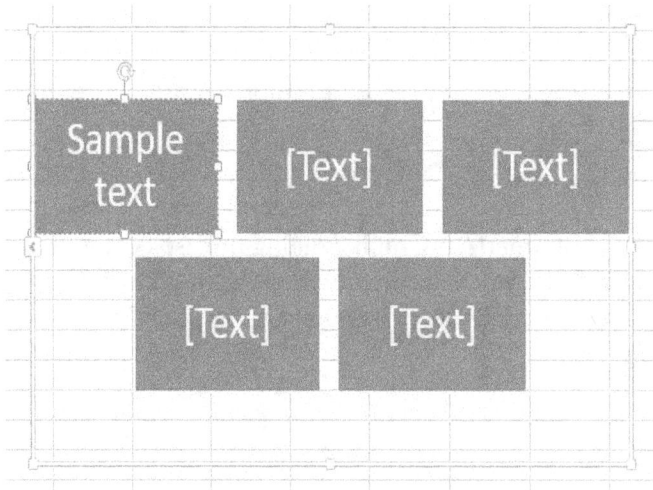

You can simply click on one of the boxes and type in your text, if desired. Notice that the font sizes adjust, depending on how much text you enter.

To add text to a SmartArt graphic using the Text pane, use the following procedure.

Step 1: To the left of the SmartArt graphic you inserted, there is a small rectangle with an arrow. Click this arrow to open the Text Pane.

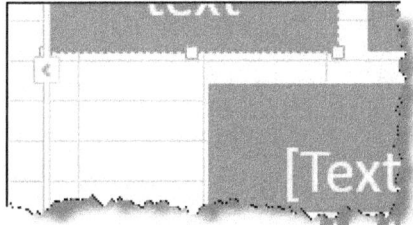

Excel opens the Text Pane.

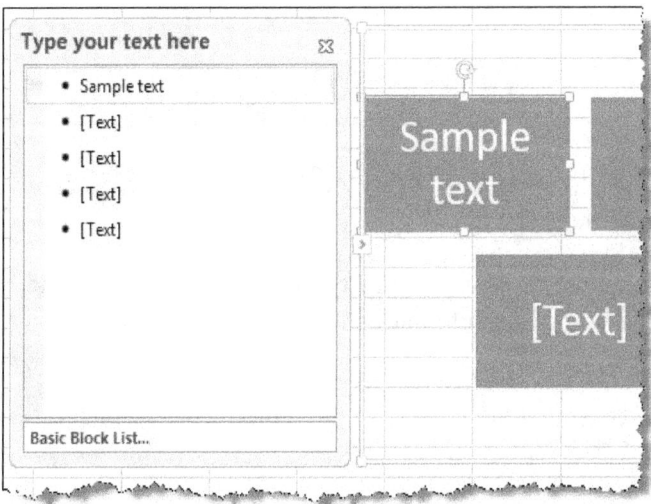

Step 2: Click on the first line and begin typing. Each line represents a new item in the graphic.

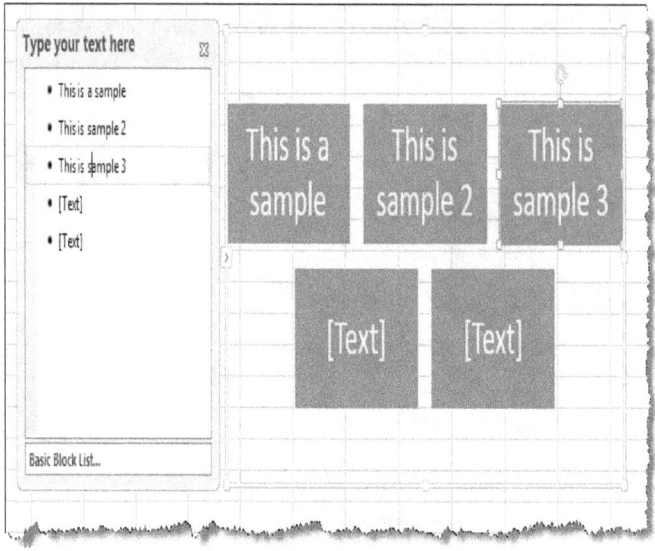

The SmartArt text adjusts to fit the graphic. The more text you enter in each graphic element, the smaller the text will become.

Step 3: When you have finished, click anywhere on the spreadsheet, and the Text Pane will close automatically. Or you can click the X in the top right corner.

Editing the Diagram

To resize a SmartArt graphic, use the following procedure.

Step 1: Select the SmartArt graphic to select it. Notice the border around the graphic.

Step 2: Select one of the corners and drag the picture. Notice the cursor changes to a diagonal line with arrows at both ends. You can make it smaller or bigger, depending on which direction you drag.

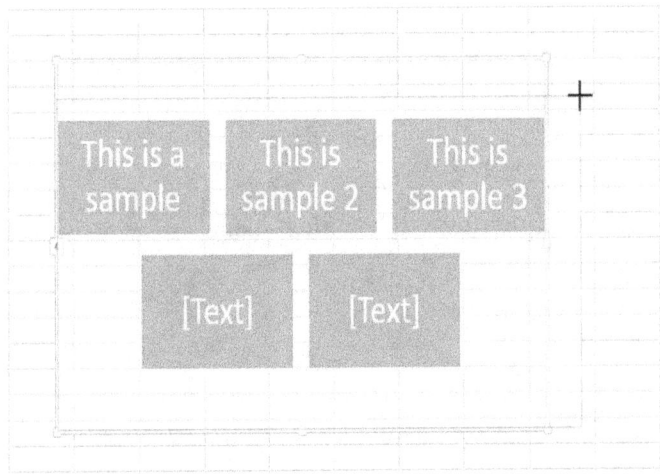

Step 3: Release the mouse when the graphic is the desired size. Notice that Excel may rearrange the graphic elements for the best look and fit.

To move the diagram, use the following procedure.

Step 1: Select the diagram border.

The cursor changes to a cross with four arrows.

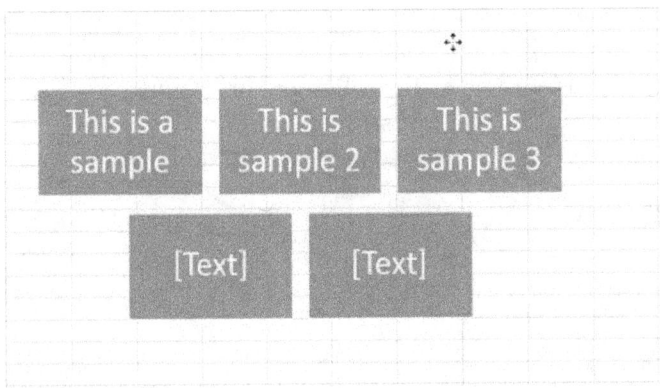

Step 2: Drag the mouse to move the diagram. Release the mouse when the diagram is in the desired location.

Note that you can move the individual parts of the SmartArt diagram using the same procedure. Just click on the individual object you want to move. Practice this for the next segment of the lesson.

Resetting the diagram allows you to quickly return the graphic to the original alignment and spacing between elements, use the following procedure to reset a diagram.

Step 1: Right-click on the diagram.

Step 2: Select **Reset Graphic** from the context menu.

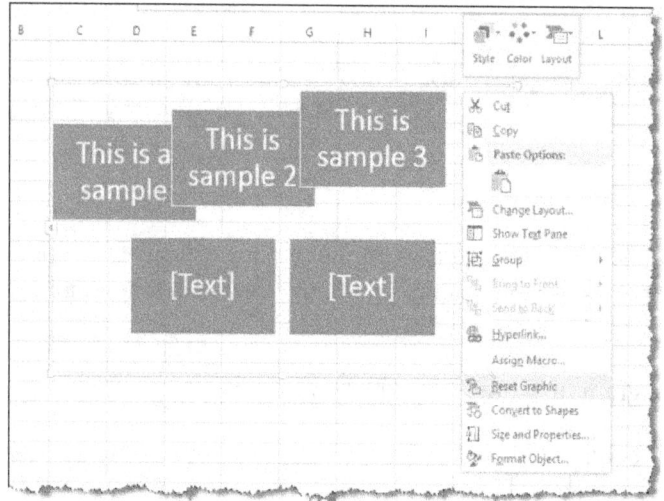

Adding Pictures

To insert a picture from a file, use the following procedure.

Step 1: Select the **Insert** tab from the Ribbon.

Step 2: Select **Picture**.

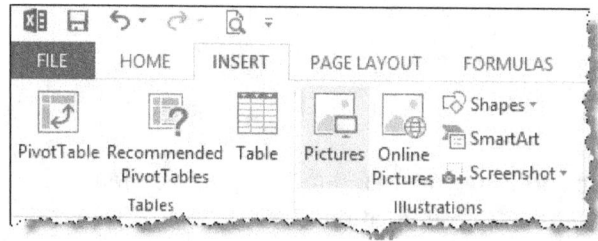

Step 3: Navigate to the location of the file and highlight the file you want to insert.

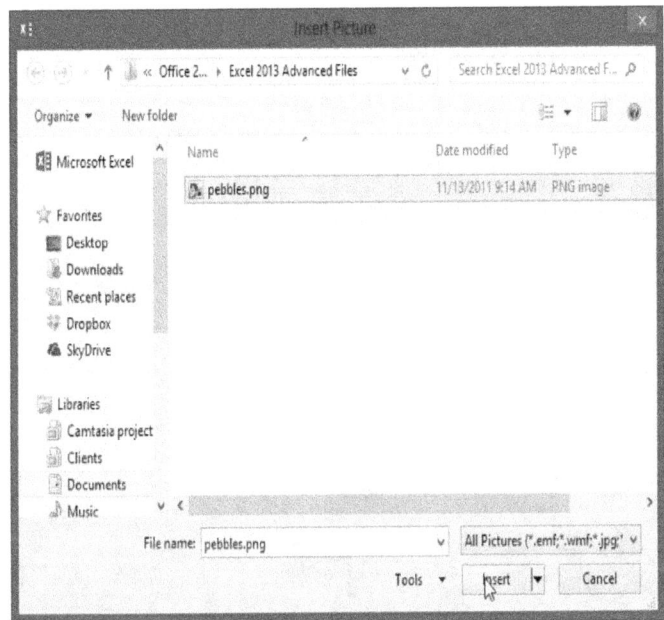

Step 4: Select **Insert**.

Excel inserts the picture.

To insert an online picture, use the following procedure.

Step 1: Select the **Insert** tab from the Ribbon.

Step 2: Select **Online Pictures**.

Step 3: In the *Insert Pictures* dialog box, select the place where you want to search for images.

Step 4: Enter a search term. Press Enter to begin searching.

Step 5: Excel displays the matching images. To insert one, double-click it or highlight it and select **Insert**.

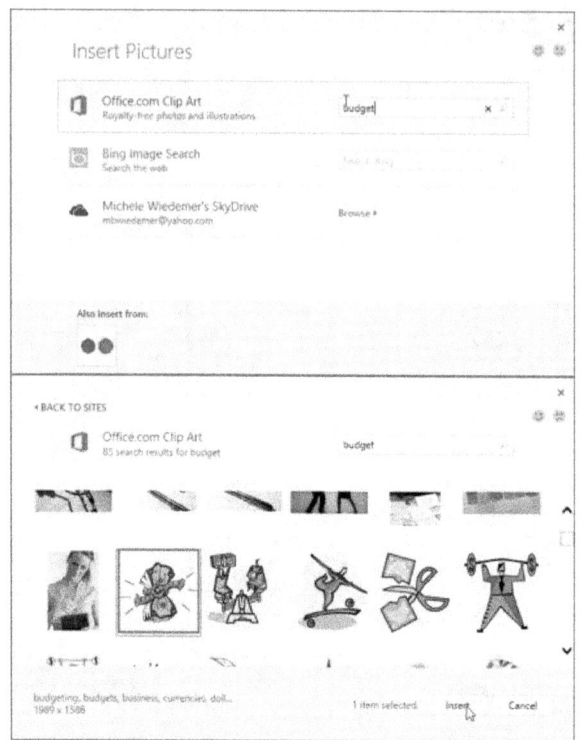

To insert a full size screenshot, use the following procedure.

Step 1: Select the **Insert** tab from the Ribbon.

Step 2: Select **Screenshot**.

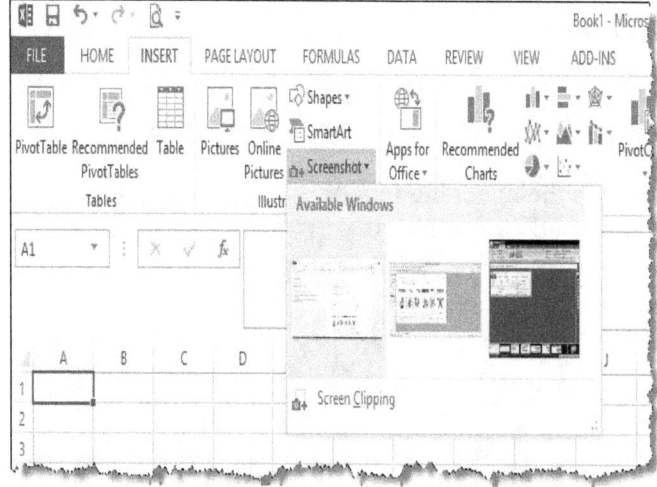

Step 3: The Screenshot gallery includes a thumbnail image of other windows you have open. Select the image that you want to insert.

Excel inserts the image.

To insert a screen clipping, use the following procedure.

Step 1: Make sure that the area of the screen you want is ready to capture. Excel will automatically return to the previous window for a screen clipping.

Step 2: Select the **Insert** tab from the Ribbon.

Step 3: Select **Screenshot**.

Step 4: Select **Screen Clipping**.

Step 5: Drag the mouse to capture the area of the screen that you want to insert in your presentation. The screen is slightly greyed out, except for the area you are capturing.

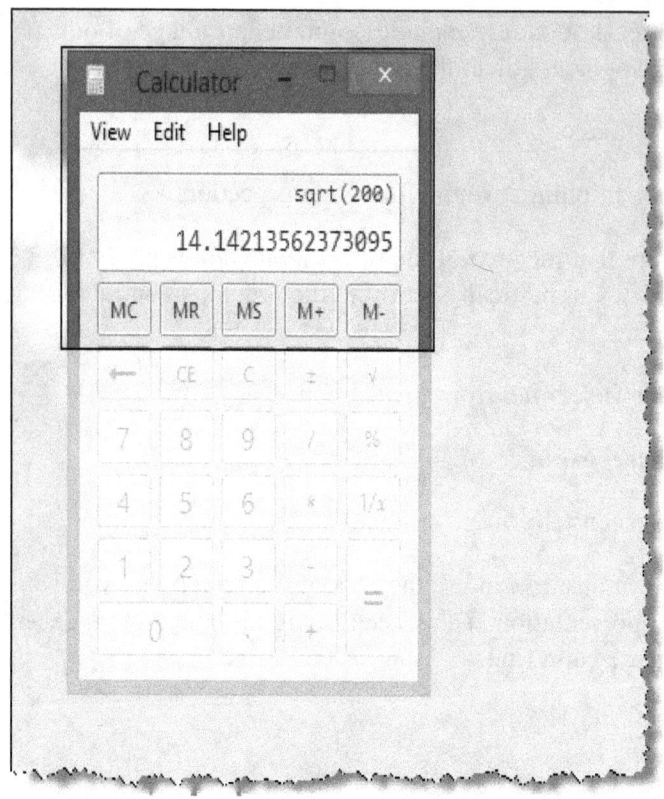

Step 6: When you release your mouse, Excel inserts the screen clipping into the workbook at the current cursor position.

Adding Text Boxes

To insert a text box, use the following procedure.

Step 1: Select the **Insert** tab from the Ribbon.

Step 2: Select **Text Box**. Select **Horizontal Text Box** or **Vertical Text Box**.

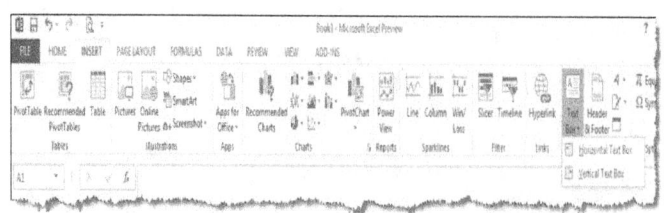

Step 3: Click on the worksheet and drag the mouse to draw the text box.

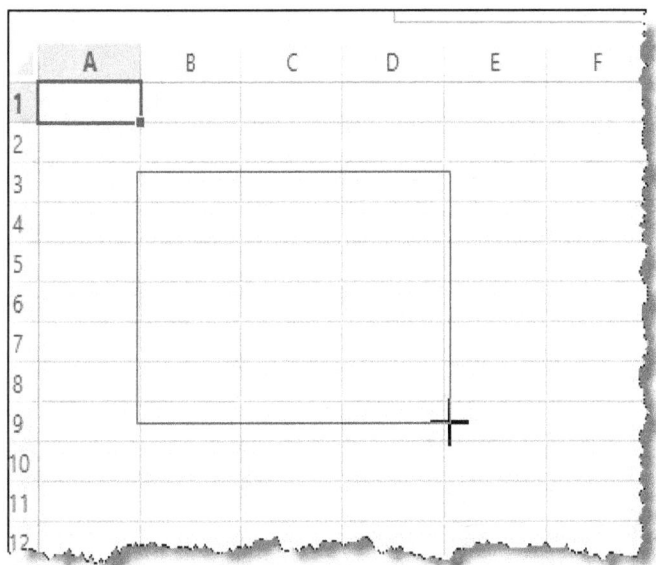

Step 4: When you release the mouse, Excel inserts the text box.

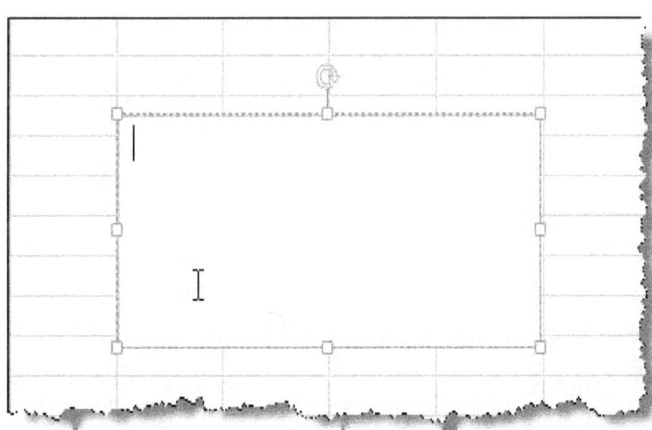

Step 5: Begin typing to enter text into the text box.

Drawing Shapes

To draw a shape, use the following procedure.

Step 1: Select the **Insert** tab from the Ribbon.

Step 2: Select **Shapes**.

Excel displays the Shapes gallery.

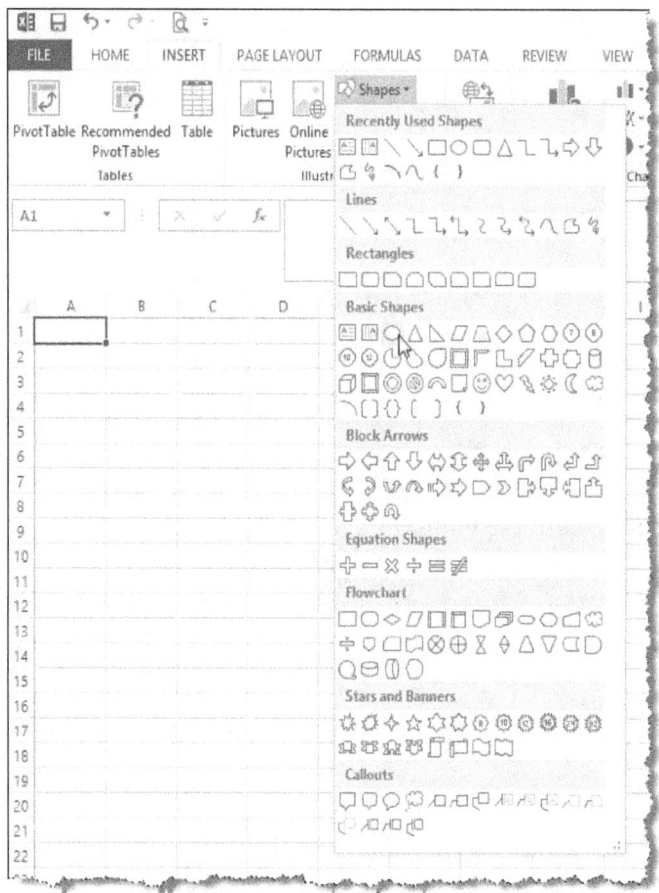

Step 3: Select a shape tool.

Step 4: Drag the mouse in the desired location to create the selected shape. The cursor is a cross while you are drawing.

Step 5: Release the mouse to complete the shape.

About the Contextual Tabs

The Tools tabs for working with SmartArt.

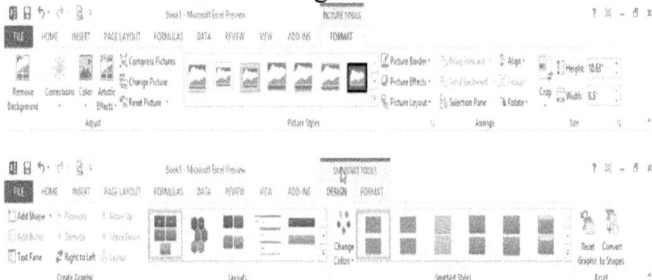

The Tools tab for working with pictures.

The Tools tab for working with a Text box or shape.

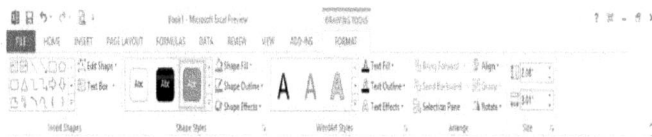

Chapter 3 – Auditing

This chapter introduces concepts that will help you troubleshoot formulas as we progress through the course. Precedent cells are cells whose contents are used in the active cell. Dependent cells are used in other cells contents or formulas. This chapter explains how to show these relationships. It also explains how to display the formulas, instead of the results, in a worksheet. You will also learn how to work with comments in this chapter.

Tracing Precedent Cells

To trace precedents, use the following procedure.

Step 1: Select the cell that contains the formula you want to trace. Cell D18 is used in this example.

Step 2: Select the **Formulas** tab from the Ribbon.

Step 3: Select **Trace Precedents**.

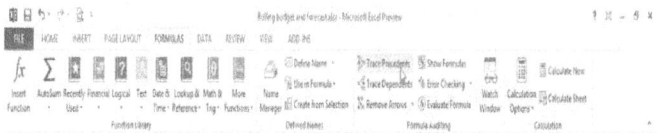

Step 4: Excel adds a tracer arrow from each cell that provides data to the active cell.

Line Item	February	
PROFIT AND LOSS		
Revenue		
Budget	$75,000	$
Actual	$70,000	$
Budget variance (Actual – Budget)	($5,000)	$
Prior year	$60,000	$
Prior year variance (Actual – Prior year)	$10,000	$
Cost of Goods Sold		
	$55,000	

To remove the tracers, select **Remove Arrows**.

Tracing the Dependents of a Cell

To trace dependents, use the following procedure.

Step 1: Select the cell that you want to trace. Cell D18 is used in this example.

Step 2: Select the **Formulas** tab from the Ribbon.

Step 3: Select **Trace Dependents**.

Step 4: Excel adds a tracer arrow to each cell that uses the active cell's data.

Step 5: Click the Trace Dependents tool again to see further relationships that are influenced by the active cell's contents.

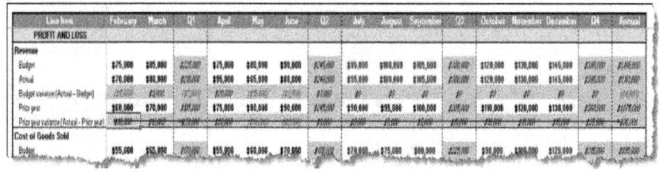

Displaying Formulas Within the Sheet

To display formulas within the sheet, use the following procedure.

Step 1: Select the **Formulas** tab from the Ribbon.

Step 2: Select **Show Formulas**.

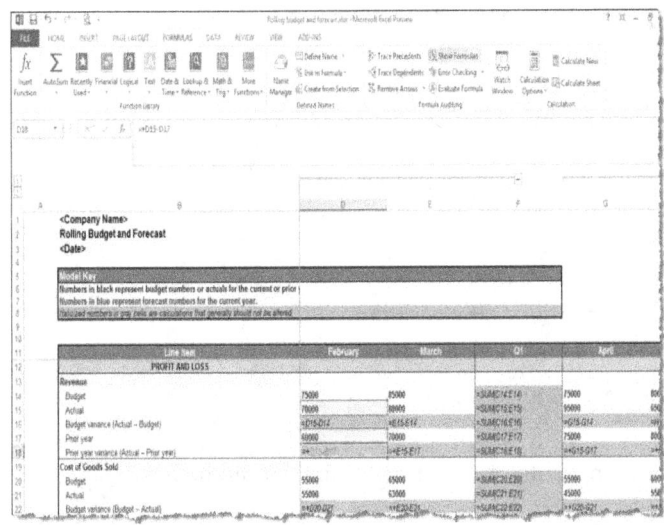

Excel expands the cells as necessary and displays all the worksheet's formulas in their cells.

Adding, Displaying, Editing, and Removing Comments

To add a comment, use the following procedure.

Step 1: Select the cell where you want to add a comment.

Step 2: Select the **Review** tab from the Ribbon.

Step 3: Select **New Comment**.

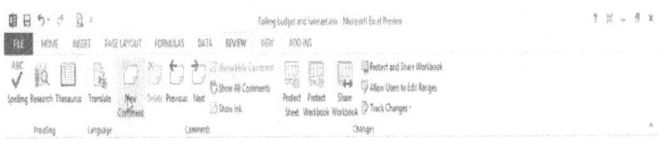

Step 4: Begin typing your comment.

Q1	April	May
$218,000	$95,000	$65,000
($7,000)	$20,000	($15,000)
$185,000		
$33,000		
$170,000		
$165,500	$45,000	$55,000
$4,500	$10,000	$5,000
$147,000	$49,000	$51,000

Sample comment

To show or hide comments, use the following procedure.

Step 1: Select the cell with the comment.

Step 2: Select Show/Hide Comment or Show All Comments.

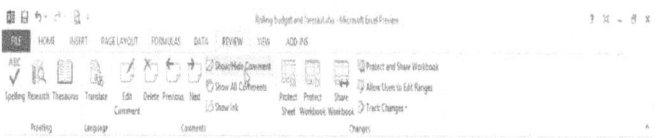

To edit a comment, use the following procedure.

Step 1: Select the cell with the comment.

Step 2: Select Edit Comment.

Excel opens the comment for editing. You can select text to change it, delete, or add text to the comment.

Q1	April	May
$218,000	$95,000	$65,000
($7,000)	$20,000	($15,000)
$185,000		
$33,000	Sample comment	
$170,000		
$165,500	$45,000	$55,000
$4,500	$10,000	$5,000
$147,000	$49,000	$51,000

To remove a comment, use the following procedure.

Step 1: Select the cell with the comment.

Step 2: Select **Delete** from the Review tab on the Ribbon.

Chapter 4 – Creating Charts

Charts provide a visual way of relating information. We will start with a new feature in 2013: Recommended Charts. Excel provides a customized set of charts based on data you select. This chapter will also explain how to insert a chart of your choosing. You will learn about the chart tools tab and gain an overview of the parts of a chart. Finally, you will learn how to resize and move a chart.

Using Recommended Charts

To insert a recommended chart, use the following procedure.

Step 1: Select the data that you want to use in your chart.

Step 2: Select the **Insert** tab from the Ribbon.

Step 3: Select **Recommended Charts**.

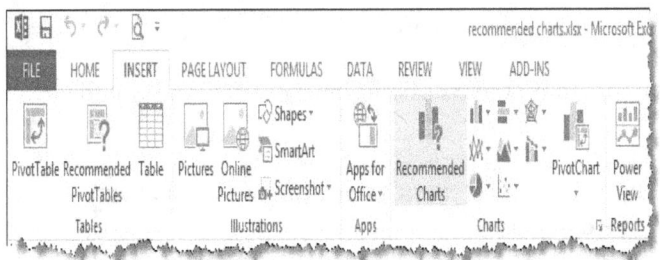

Step 4: In the *Insert Chart* dialog box, the Recommended Charts tab shows several charts that Excel recommended for the type of data you have selected. As you select each option on the left side of the dialog box, the right side shows a preview.

Step 5: When you find a chart that you want to use, select it in the list, and select **OK**.

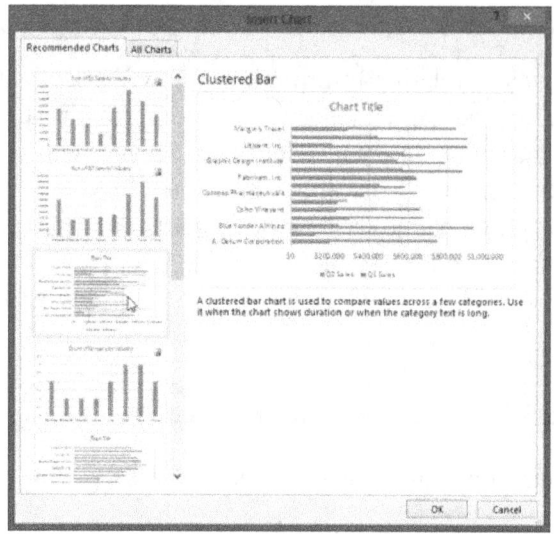

Inserting a Chart

The types of charts in Excel 2013 are:

Column charts – Column charts allow you to visually compare values across a few categories.

Line Chart – Line charts show trends over time (such as years, months, or days) or categories.

Pie charts – Pie charts show your data in proportions of a whole. The total of your numbers should be 100%. Doughnut charts are included. Donut charts are good when there are multiple series that relate to a larger sum.

Bar charts – Bar charts allow you to visually compare values across a few categories when the chart shows duration or the category text is long.

Area charts – Area charts show trends over time or categories. Use it to highlight the magnitude of change over time.

Scatter charts – Scatter or bubble charts show the relationship between sets of values.

Stock, Surface or Radar charts – This category includes a number of chart types to help you show the trend of a stock's performance over time, show trends in values in a curve or with color, or show values relative to a center point.

Combo chart – Combo charts highlight different types of information when your values vary widely or you have mixed types of data.

To insert a chart, use the following procedure.

Step 1: Select the cells, including the labels to include in the chart.

Step 2: Select the **Insert** tab from the Ribbon.

Step 3: Select the type of chart you would like to use.

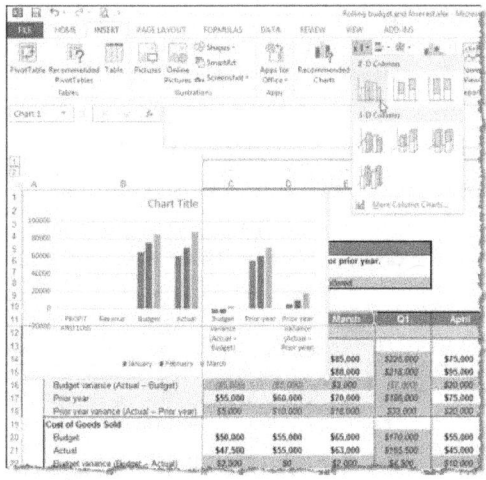

Excel displays the chart.

Overview of the Chart Tools Tabs

The Tools tabs for working with charts.

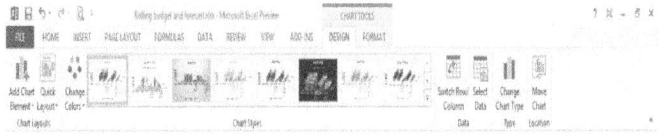

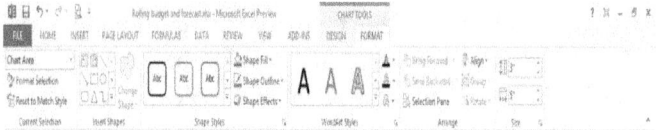

Understanding Chart Elements

The parts of a standard chart are.

- The **Chart** area includes all other parts of the chart that appear inside the chart window.

- A **data point** represents a single value in the worksheet. Depending on the type of chart, this may be a bar, a pie slice, or another shape or pattern.

- A group of related data points make up the **data series**. Charts usually have more than one data series, except pie charts, which only represents one data series.

- An **axis** is a reference line for plotting data. A two-dimensional chart has an X-axis and a y-axis. For many charts, the label is on the X-axis and the values are on the y-axis. Three dimensional charts also have a Z-axis. A pie chart does not have an axis of any type.

- A **tick mark** intersects an axis as a small line. It may have a label and can indicate a category, scale, or chart data series.

- The **Plot area** includes all axes and data point markers.

- **Gridlines** can make it easier to view data values by extending tick marks across the whole plot area.

- You can add **text** to include a label or title. The text can be attached to the chart or axis, which cannot be moved independently of the chart. Unattached text is a text box simply shown with the chart.

- The **legend** defines the patterns, colors, or symbols used in the data markers.

Resizing and Moving the Chart

To resize a chart, use the following procedure.

Step 1: Click on the chart to select it. Notice the border around the chart.

Step 2: Select one of the corners and drag the chart. Notice the cursor changes to a diagonal line with arrows at both ends. You can make it smaller or bigger, depending on which direction you drag.

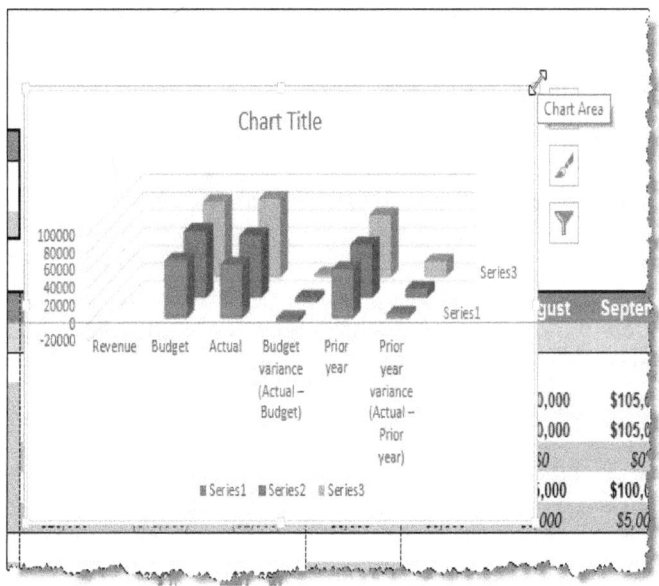

Step 3: Release the mouse when the chart is the desired size.

To move the chart to a new worksheet in the workbook, use the following procedure.

Step 1: Select the chart.

Step 2: Select the **Chart Tools Design** tab.

Step 3: Select the **Move Chart** tool.

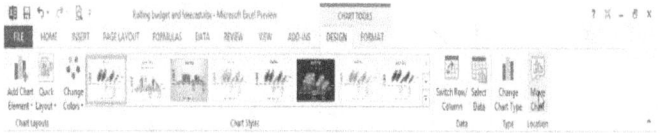

Excel displays the Move Chart dialog box.

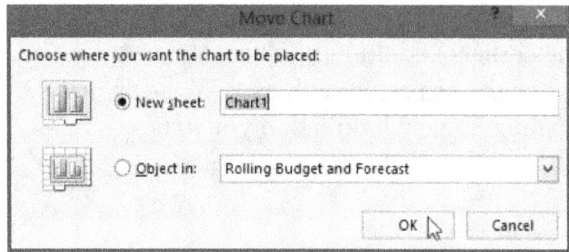

Step 4: Select **New Sheet**.

Step 5: Give the new worksheet a new name, if desired.

Step 6: Select **OK**.

Excel creates a new worksheet in the workbook (notice the tabs at the bottom). The chart has also been resized to fill the worksheet.

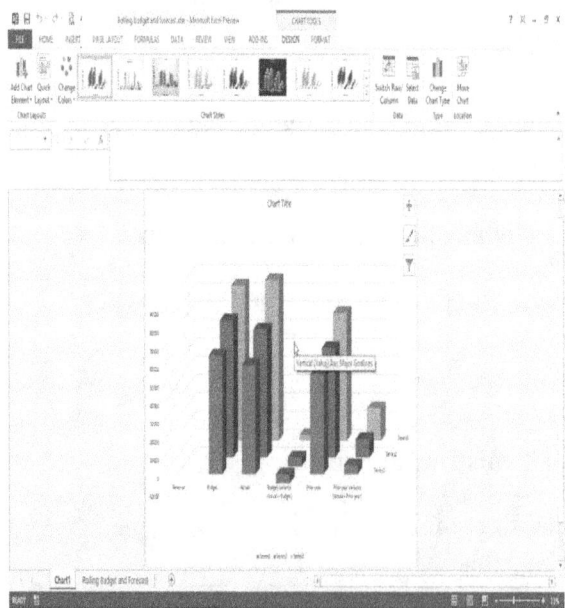

Chapter 5 – Working with Charts

Now that you have decided what type of chart to use, it is time to make your data shine. Those little icons to the right of your chart are new to Excel 2013 and will help you add chart elements, change the style and color scheme, and use data filters. You will also learn about adding and working with data labels.

Using Chart Elements

To add a chart element, use the following procedure.

Step 1: Select the + sign on the right side of your chart.

Step 2: Check the box of the element you want to add. (Or clear the box for the element you want to remove). Many of the elements include a small arrow to the right of the option. Click the arrow to see additional options.

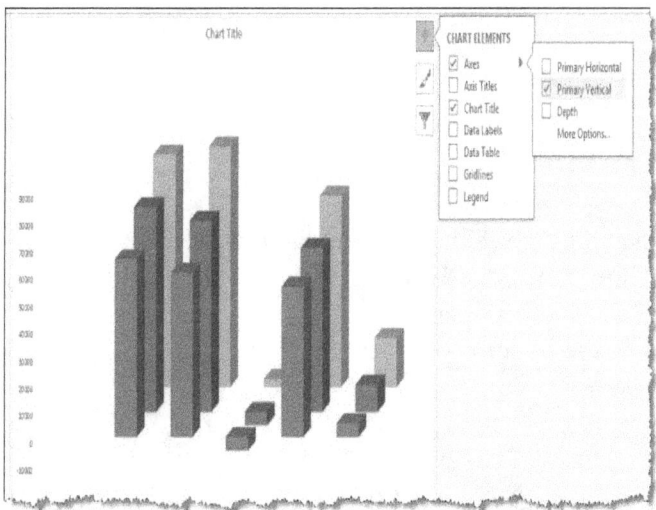

You can also use the **Add Chart Element** tool from the **Chart Tools Design** tab on the Ribbon. Pause your pointer over an option to see a preview.

To access the additional formatting options for one or more elements, use the following procedure.

Step 1: Select **More Options** from either Chart Elements list (from the icon next to the chart or the Ribbon).

Step 2: The *Format* pane opens for the selected element.

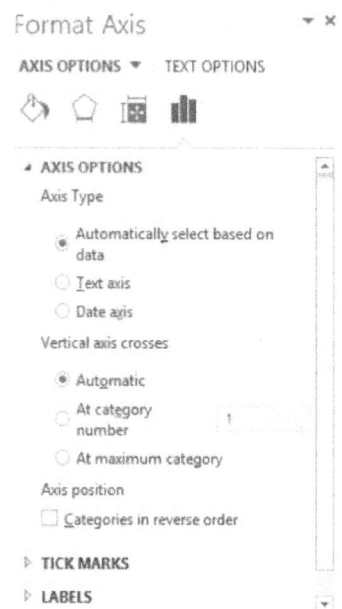

Select each of the icons to see the different options, such as Fill and Line; Shadow, Glow Soft Edges and 3-D Format; Alignment; Text Fill and Outline, and more, depending on which element you selected. You can then view the options for other elements.

Using Chart Styles and Colors

To select a new chart style, use the following procedure.

Step 1: Select the chart you want to format.

Step 2: Select the paintbrush icon to the right of your chart.

Step 3: Select the desired chart style.

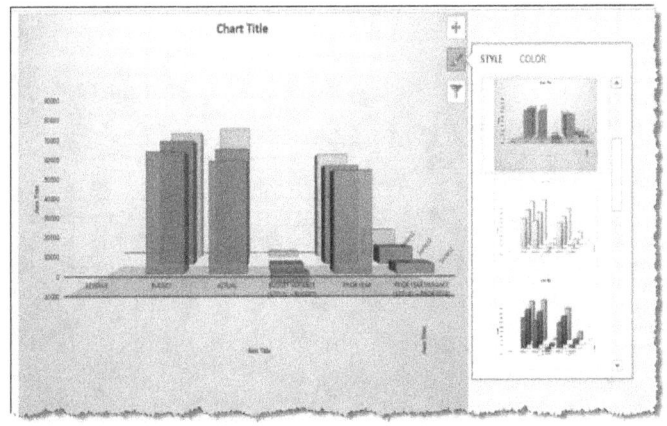

To select new chart colors, use the following procedure.

Step 1: Select the chart you want to format.

Step 2: Select the paintbrush icon to the right of your chart.

Step 3: Select the **Color** tab.

Step 4: Select the desired color palate.

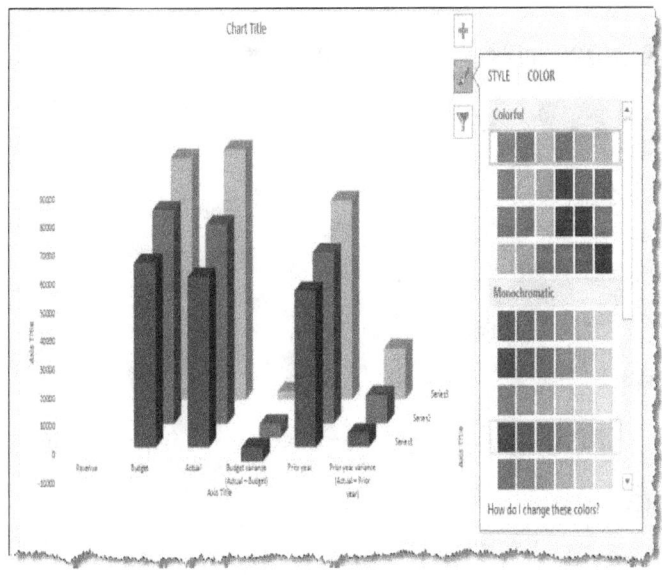

Using Chart Filters

Step 1: Select the funnel sign on the right side of your chart.

Step 2: Check the box of the value you want to add. (Or clear the box for the value you want to remove).

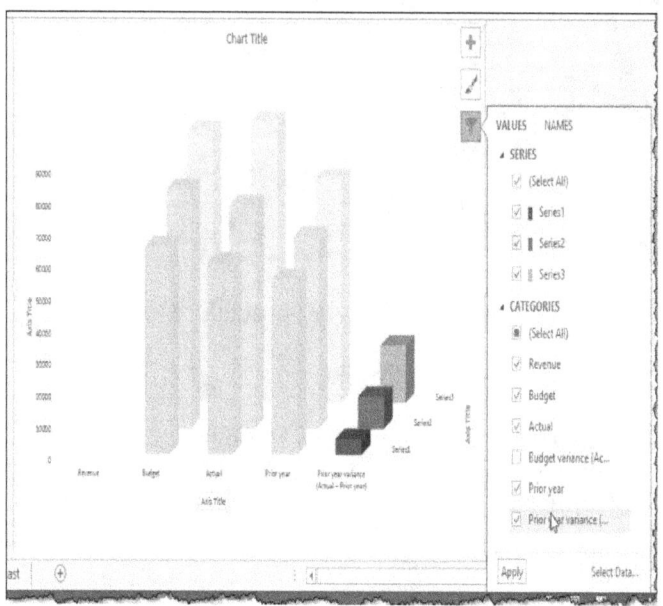

Step 3: To edit a Series name, select the worksheet icon next to the series.

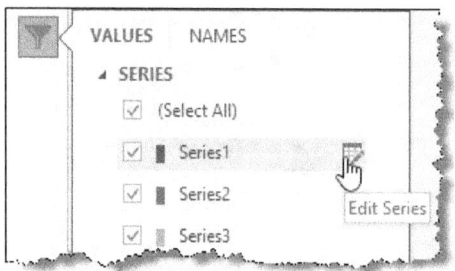

Step 4: In the *Edit Series* dialog box, enter the name you want to use.

Step 5: Select **OK**.

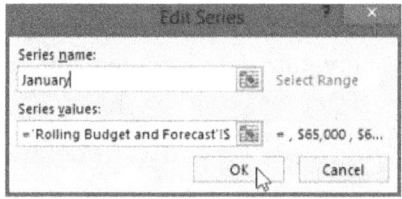

Working with Data Labels

To add data labels to a chart, use the following procedure.

Step 1: Select the chart that you want to label. Select the data series (such as one group of columns) or an individual data point to label, if desired.

Step 2: Select the + sign to the right of the chart.

Step 3: Check the **Data Labels** box and select an option from the list to the right, if desired. The options are different, based on which type of chart you have or which type of data point or series you selected.

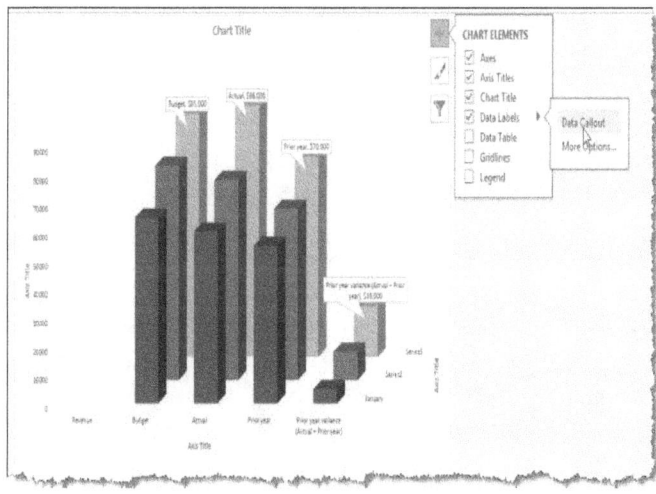

To format data labels, use the following procedure.

Step 1: Select the chart that you want to label. Select the data series (such as one group of columns) or an individual data point to label, if desired.

Step 2: Select the + sign to the right of the chart.

Step 3: Select the small arrow to the right of **Data Labels**.

Step 4: Select **More Options**.

Step 5: In the *Format Data Labels* pane, you can set the Fill, Border, Effects, Size & Properties, Label Options, Text Fill, Text Effects, and Text Box options. Review each of these views of the Format Data Labels pane. Note that each set of options can be expanded or condensed using the small arrow to the left of the title.

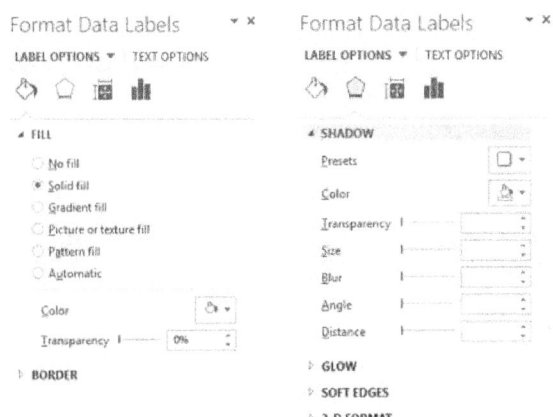

Format Data Labels ▾ ×

LABEL OPTIONS ▾   TEXT OPTIONS

⌖ ⬠ ▦ ▥

▲ FILL

○ No fill
● Solid fill
○ Gradient fill
○ Picture or texture fill
○ Pattern fill
○ Automatic

Color   ◌ ▾
Transparency |——— 0%

▷ BORDER

Format Data Labels ▾ ×

LABEL OPTIONS ▾   TEXT OPTIONS

⌖ ⬠ ▦ ▥

▲ SHADOW

Presets   ▢ ▾
Color   ◌ ▾
Transparency |——
Size |——
Blur |——
Angle |——
Distance |——

▷ GLOW
▷ SOFT EDGES
▷ 3-D FORMAT

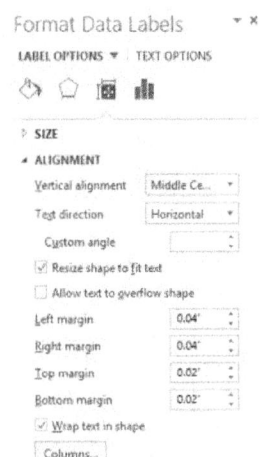

Format Data Labels ▾ ×

LABEL OPTIONS ▾   TEXT OPTIONS

⌖ ⬠ ▦ ▥

▷ SIZE
▲ ALIGNMENT

Vertical alignment   Middle Ce... ▾
Text direction   Horizontal   ▾
Custom angle
☑ Resize shape to fit text
☐ Allow text to overflow shape
Left margin   0.04"
Right margin   0.04"
Top margin   0.02"
Bottom margin   0.02"
☑ Wrap text in shape
Columns...

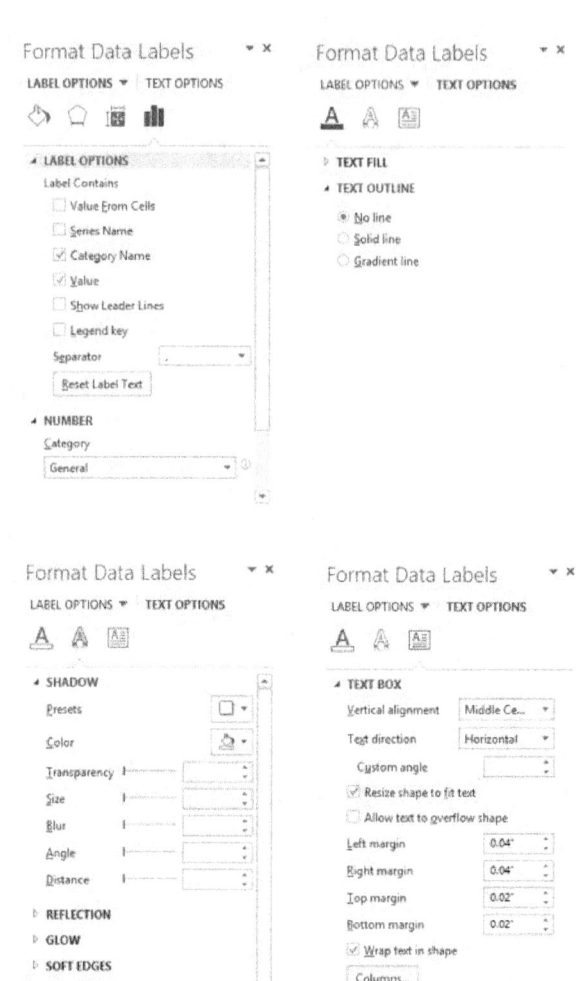

Chapter 6 – Creating Pivot Tables and Pivot Charts

PivotTables allow you to analyze numeric data in depth. You can use this tool to answer unanticipated questions about data. PivotTables are interactive, cross-tabulated Excel reports that summarize and analyze data. In this chapter, you will learn how to insert a Pivot Table using Excel Recommendations. You will also learn how to choose fields and group data to create different types of Pivot Tables. You will gain an understanding of the PivotTable Tools tab. You will also learn how to change the data displayed and refresh the table. You will also learn how to create a PivotChart, both from an existing PivotTable and straight from data. Finally, we will look at some real-life examples of using PivotTables and PivotCharts.

Inserting a PivotTable using Excel Recommendations

To insert a PivotTable from recommendations, use the following procedure.

Step 1: Highlight the data you want to analyze.

Step 2: Select the **Insert** tab from the Ribbon.

Step 3: Select **Recommended PivotTables**.

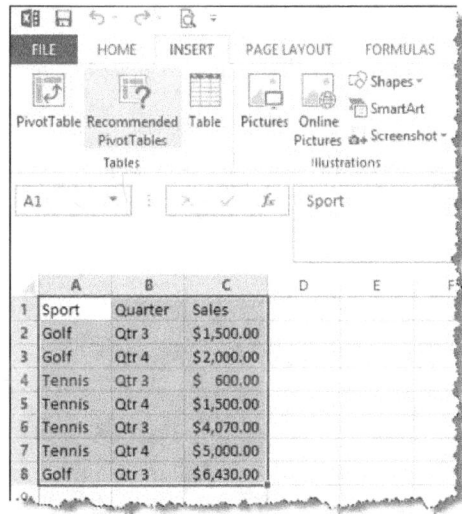

Excel displays the Recommended PivotTables dialog box.

Step 4: Select the Pivot Table you want to use from the choices on the left side of the dialog box. You can see a preview on the right.

Step 5: Select **OK**.

Excel displays your PivotTable on a new worksheet.

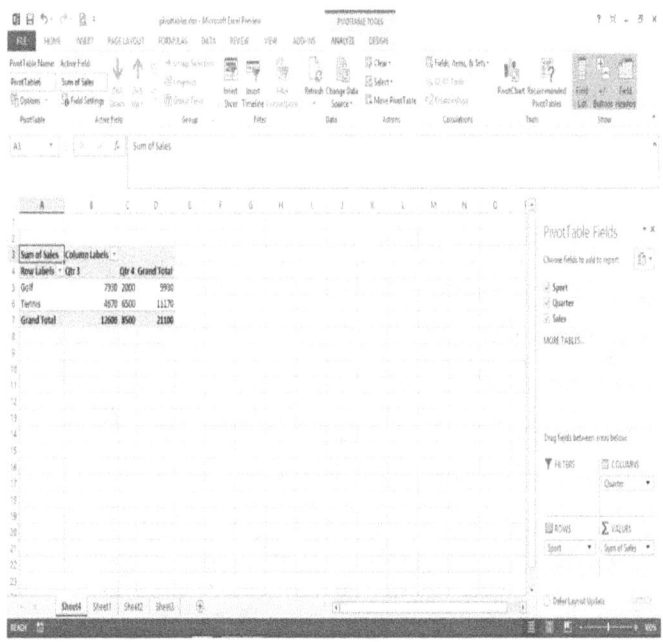

Choosing Fields and Grouping Data

To add (or remove) fields to/from the PivotTable report, use the following procedure.

Step 1: Check the box next to a field listed in the PivotTable Fields pane to include it in the report. Clear a box to remove it. The default location where fields are added are as follows:

- Nonnumeric fields are added to the Row Labels.

- Numerical fields are added to the Values area.

- Date and time values are added to the Column Labels.

You can also apply a filter or sorting to one or more fields, by selecting the small arrow to the far right of the field name.

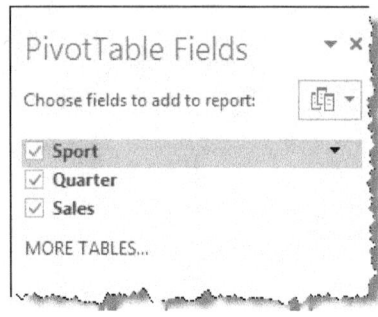

The bottom of the PivotTable Field List pane includes four areas:

- Filters

- Rows

- Columns

- Values

To group the data, use the following procedure.

Step 1: Right click on a field label in the PivotTable Field List and select one of the options from the context menu.

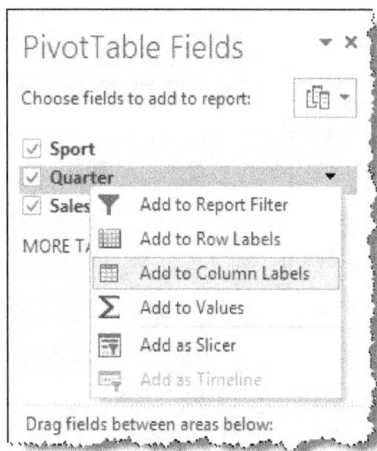

Step 2: You can also simply drag the fields from one area to another. You can even drag a field from the top portion of the pane to one of the bottom areas.

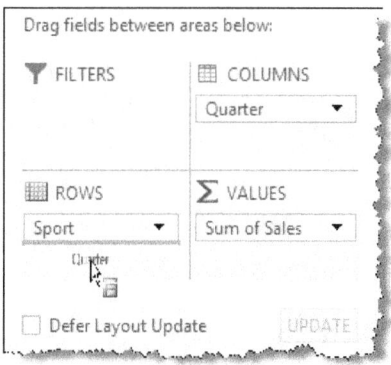

Overview of the Pivot Table Tools Tabs

The Tools tabs for working with PivotTables.

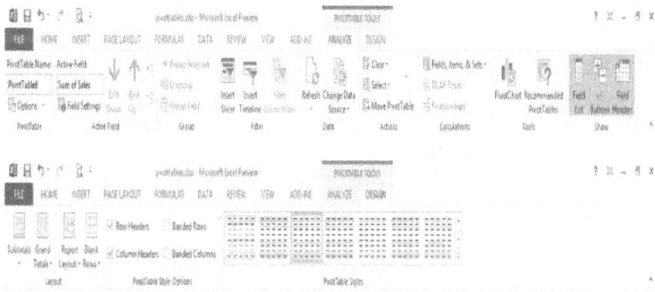

Changing the Data Displayed and Refreshing the PivotTable

To refresh the PivotTable after making a change to the data, use the following procedure.

Step 1: Return to the worksheet containing the PivotTable.

Step 2: Click somewhere on the PivotTable.

Step 3: Select the **Options** tab from the Ribbon.

Step 4: Select **Refresh**.

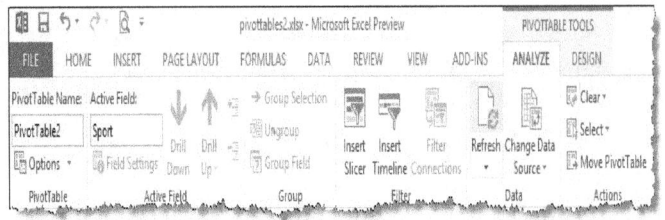

To change the data source, use the following procedure.

Step 1: Select the **PivotTable Tools Analyze** tab from the Ribbon.

Step 2: Select **Change Data Source**.

Excel returns to the worksheet of the source data and highlights the current data source. It also displays the *Change PivotTable Data Source* dialog box.

Step 3: Highlight the new data area on the worksheet.

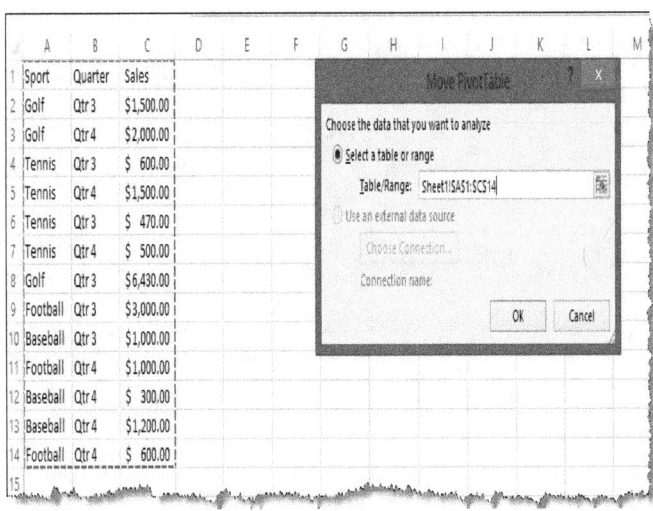

Step 4: Select **OK**.

Step 5: Excel opens the new PivotTable. Select and group the fields as desired.

Creating a Pivot Chart from a Pivot Table or Data

To add a PivotChart from a PivotTable, use the following procedure.

Step 1: Click anywhere in the PivotTable for which you want to add a chart.

Step 2: Select the **PivotTable Tools Analyze** tab from the Ribbon.

Step 3: Select **PivotChart**.

Excel displays the *Insert Chart* dialog box.

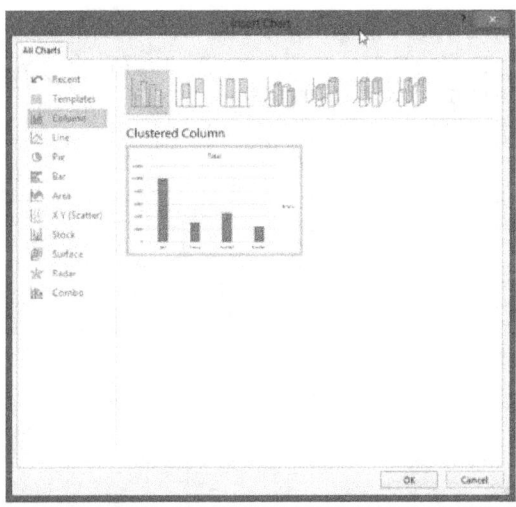

Step 4: Select the desired type of chart and select **OK**.

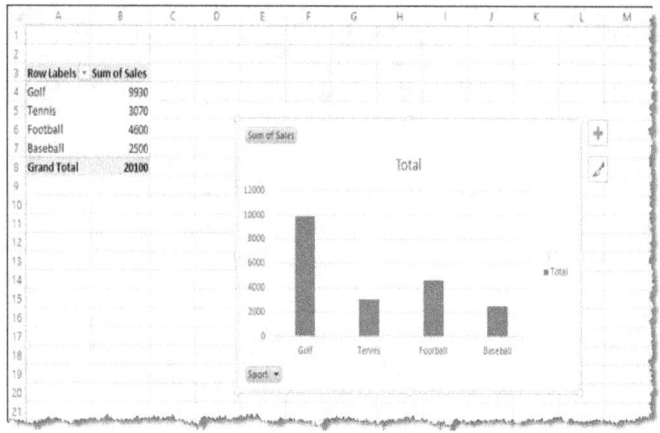

To insert a PivotChart from data, use the following procedure.

Step 1: Place your cursor somewhere in the data you want to analyze.

Step 2: Select the **Insert** tab from the Ribbon.

Step 3: Select **PivotChart**.

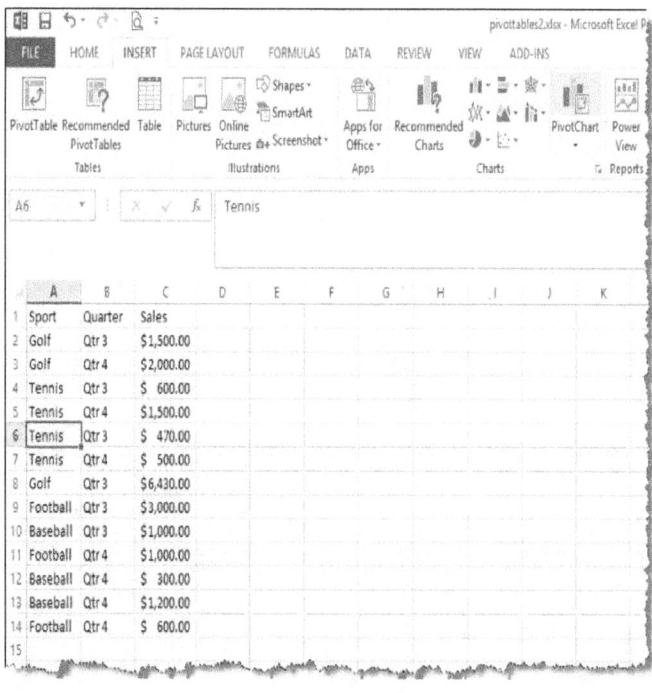

Excel displays the Create PivotChart dialog box.

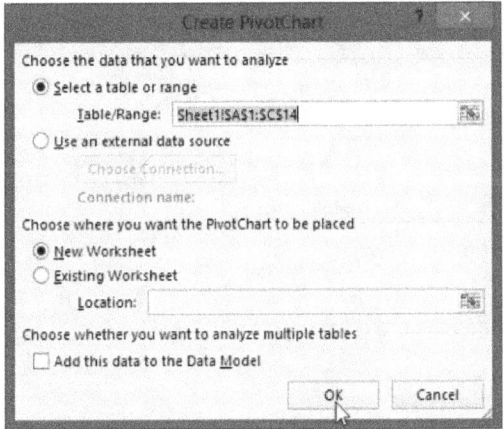

Step 4: Excel automatically provides a range of cells based on your selection. You can change the table or range if desired.

Step 5: Select a location for the PivotChart. You can have Excel create a new worksheet or select one of the existing sheets.

Step 6: Select **OK**.

Excel displays the blank PivotChart and the Fields pane for you to begin choosing your fields and grouping data.

Step 7: Add fields to view the chart.

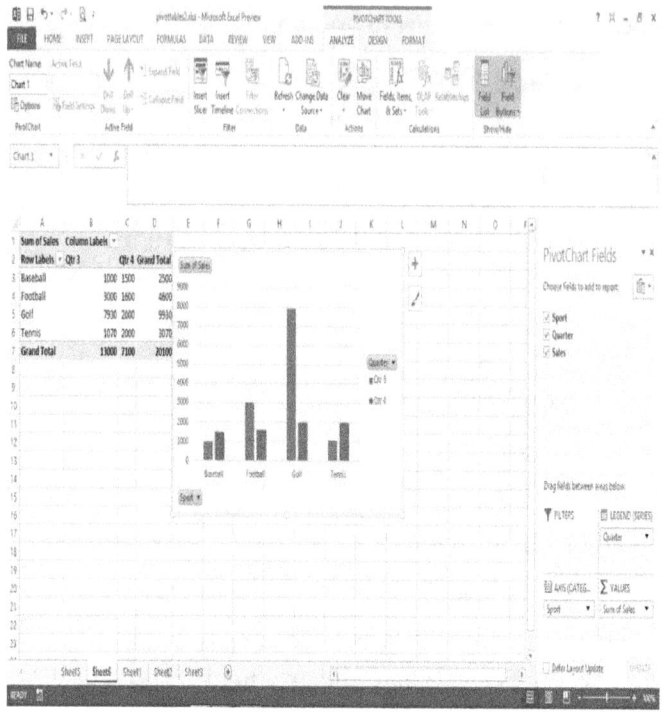

Some Real-life Examples

Find out the sum of payments from each client.

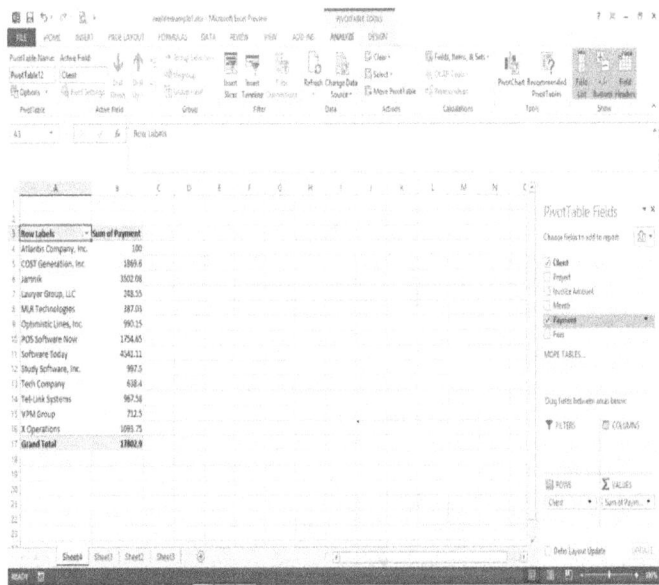

Find out the sum of payments by month.

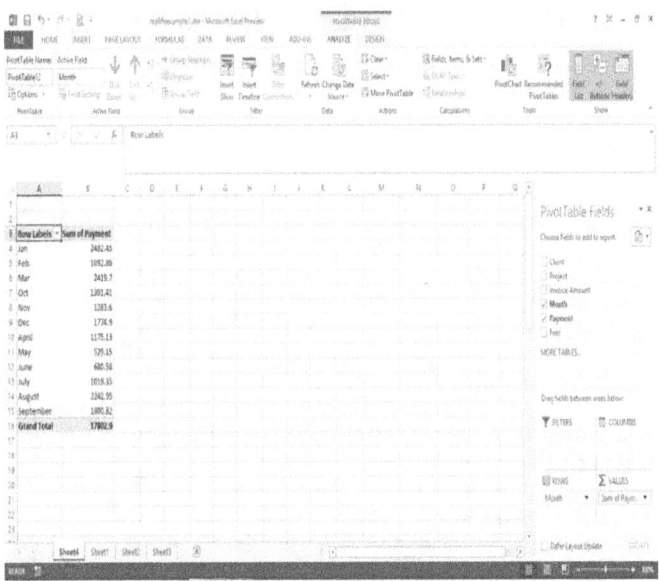

If you create a PivotTable that includes the Salesperson and the Order Amount, you get this.

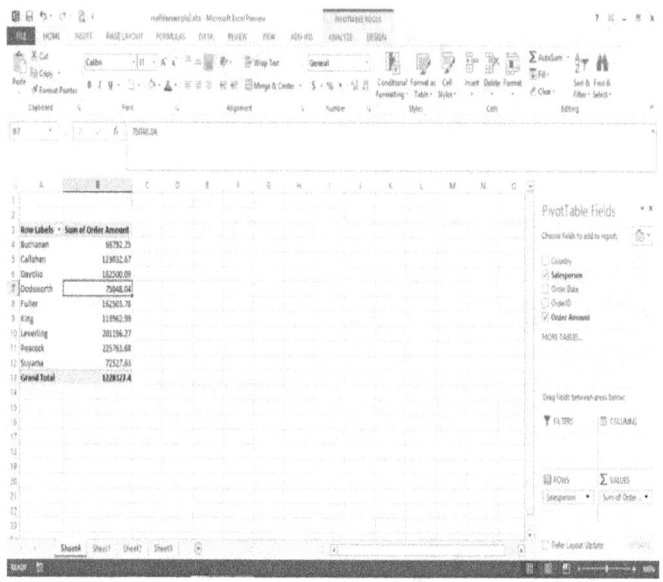

Who are the top ten salesmen?

Click the arrow next to **Row labels** and select **More Sort Options**.

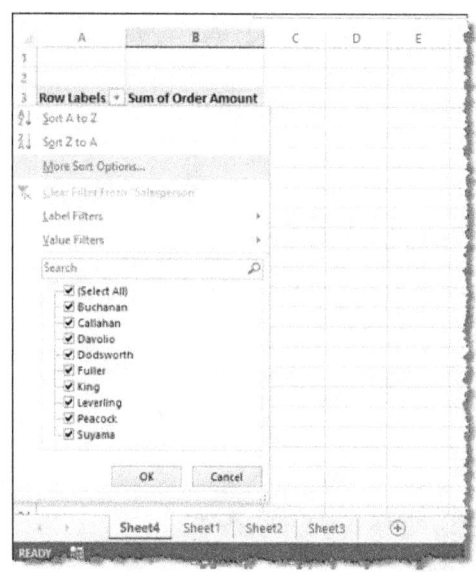

In the *Sort* dialog box, select **Ascending (A to Z)** by **Sum of Order Amount** and select OK.

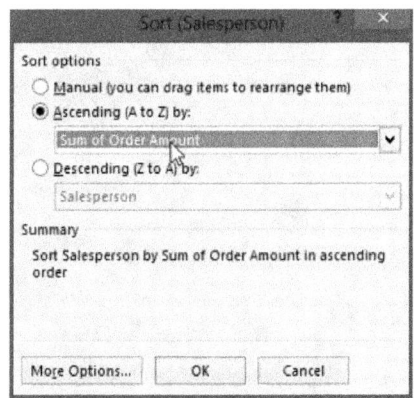

Chapter 7 – Macros

A macro is a set of recorded computer instructions. These instructions are associated with a shortcut key or macro name that makes it easy to tell your computer to run that set of instructions. This chapter will explain how to save time with macros. You will learn how to display the Developer tab, which contains the tools you will need to record macros. You will learn how to record and run macros. This chapter also explains macro security levels to avoid allowing malicious content to damage your computer with macros. Finally, you will learn how to customize and change the Quick Access Toolbar so that you have instant access to your favorite macros.

Displaying the Developer Tab

To display the Develop tab, use the following procedure.

Step 1: Select the **File** tab from the Ribbon.

Step 2: Select **Options**.

Step 3: Select **Customize the Ribbon**.

Step 4: In the **Customize the Ribbon** list on the right, check the **Developer** box.

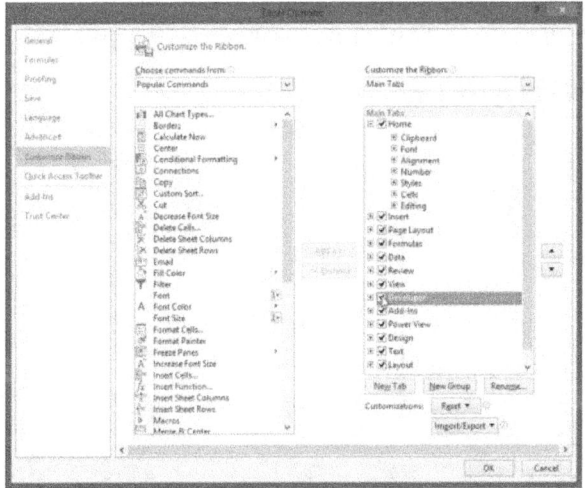

Step 5: Select **OK**.

The **Developer** tab.

Recording and Running Macros

To record a macro, use the following procedure. In this example, we will sum the column and add formatting to the numbers.

Step 1: Select the **Developer** tab from the Ribbon.

Step 2: Select **Use Relative References**.

Step 3: Select **Record Macro**.

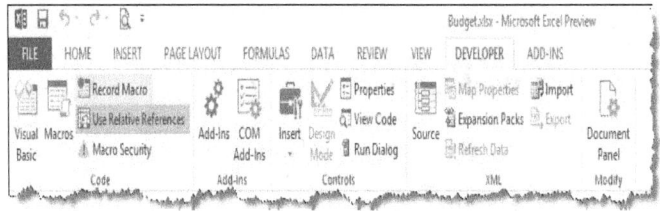

Step 4: In the *Record Macro* dialog box, give your macro a name.

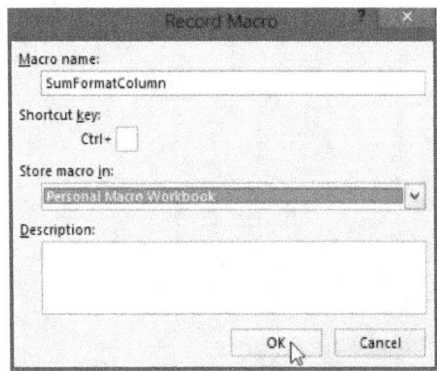

Step 5: To make the macro available to other worksheets, select **Personal Macro Workbook** from the **Store Macro In** drop down list.

Step 6: Select **OK** to begin recording.

Step 7: Perform the actions you want to record. In this example, we inserted a Sum and then formatted the total with a currency formatting and added bold face formatting.

Step 8: Select the **Developer** tab.

Step 9: Select **Stop Recording**.

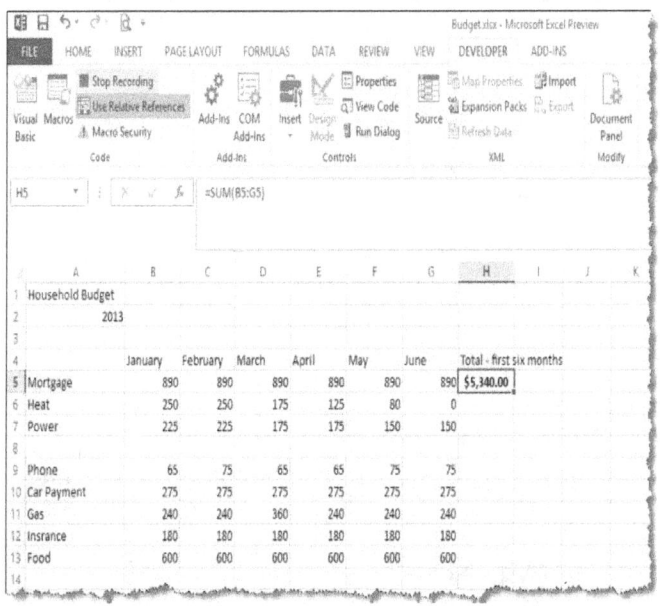

To run a macro, use the following example.

Step 1: Place your cursor in the cell where you want to perform the macro.

Step 2: Select the **Developer** tab.

Step 3: Select **Macros**.

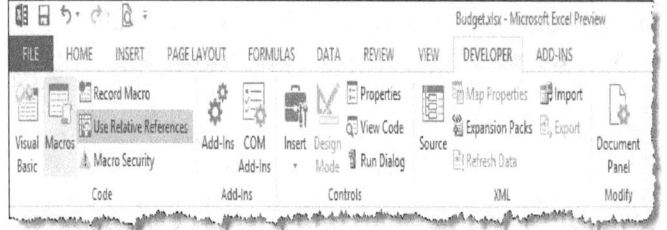

Step 4: In the *Macro* dialog box, select your macro name from the list.

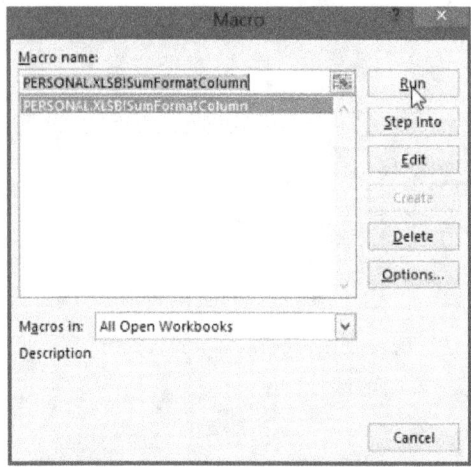

Step 5: Select **Run**.

Note that when you close Excel, you will get the following warning message.

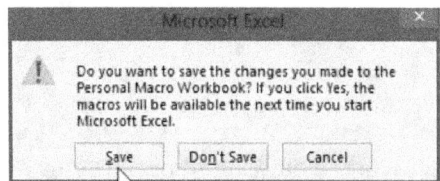

Select **Save** to keep the macro and make it available to other workbooks.

Changing the Security Level

To change the macro security, use the following procedure.

Step 1: Select the **Developer** tab.

Step 2: Select **Macro Security**.

Step 3: Select one of the following options:

Disable all macros without notification – this option only runs macros in documents in trusted locations.

Disable all macros with notification – this option disables macros that are not in trusted locations, but it provides notification, so that you can choose to enable those macros on a case by case basis.

Disable all macros except digitally signed macros – this option allows not only macros in trusted locations, but also macros that are digitally signed by a trusted publisher. Other macros are disabled with notification to allow you to choose to enable those macros on a case by case basis.

Enable all macros – this option allows all macros to run, which is potentially dangerous since virus authors often use macros to distribute malicious code on computers. Microsoft does not advise using this setting.

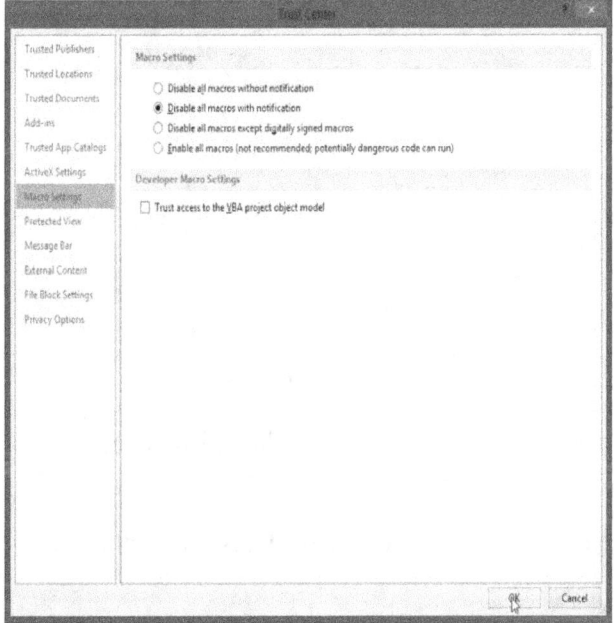

Step 4: Check the **Trust Access to the VBA Project Object Model** box only if you are a developer. This security option makes it more difficult for unauthorized programs to build code that self-replicates.

Step 5: Select **OK**.

Customizing and Changing the Quick Access Toolbar

To add a macro to the Quick Access Toolbar, use the following procedure.

Step 1: Select the arrow to the right of the Quick Access Toolbar.

Step 2: Select **More Commands**.

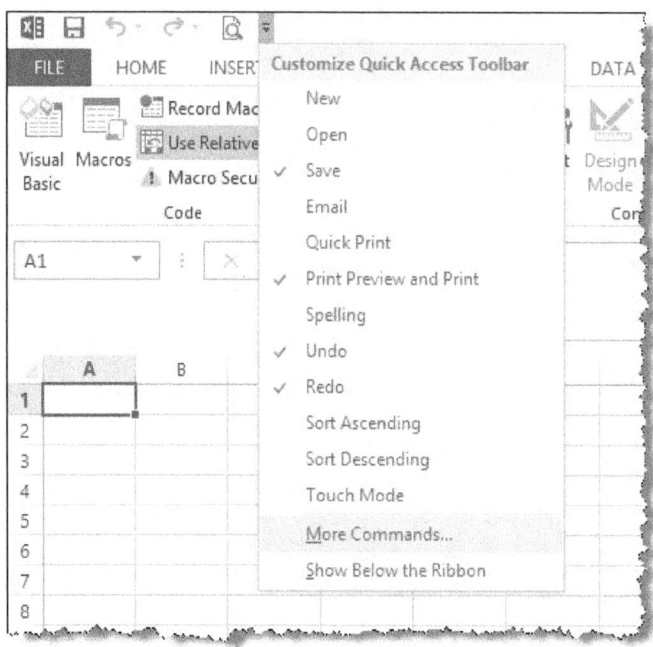

Step 3: In the **Choose Command From** drop down list, select **Macros**.

Step 4: The macro you recorded should be listed. Select it and select **Add**.

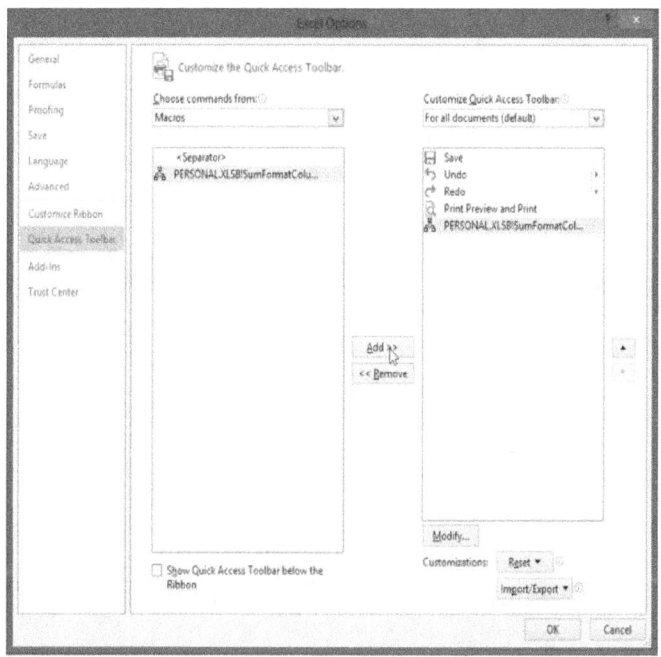

Step 5: If you would like to modify the name of the macro, select **Modify**.

Step 6: In the *Modify Button* dialog box, you can choose an icon to show in the Quick Access Toolbar. You can also modify the name.

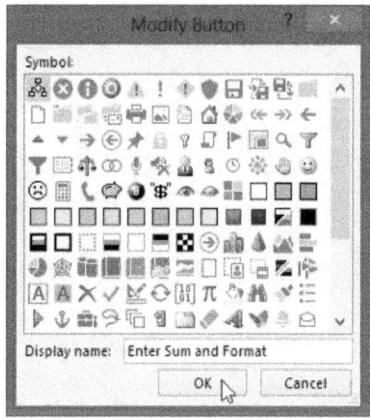

Step 7: Select **OK**.

Step 8: Select **OK** in the *Excel Options* window.

Chapter 8 – Solving Formula Errors

Formula errors can be very frustrating. This chapter will teach you how to prevent formula errors by using named ranges. You will gain an understanding of formula errors and learn how to use error checking. You will also learn how to use the Trace Errors commands. Finally, we will look at how to evaluate formulas.

Using Named Ranges

To name a range, use the following procedure.

Step 1: Highlight the cell references you want to name.

Step 2: Select the **Formulas** tab.

Step 3: Select **Define Name**.

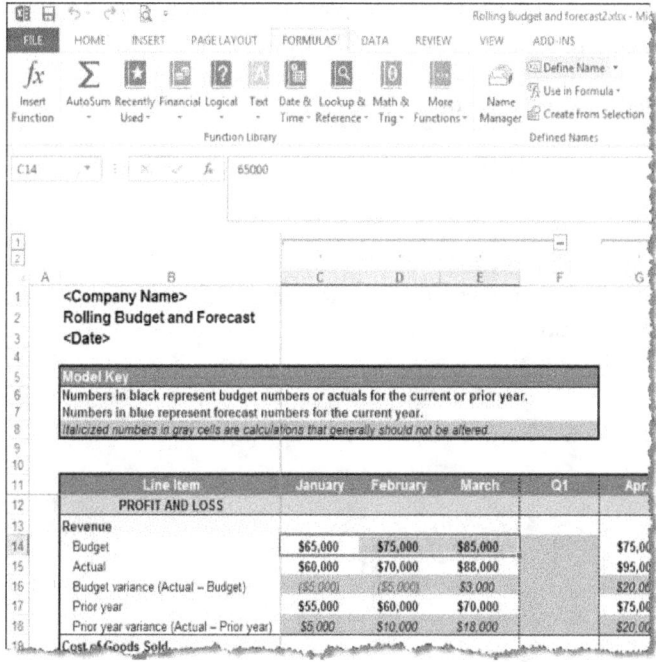

Step 4: Enter a name for the cell reference range.

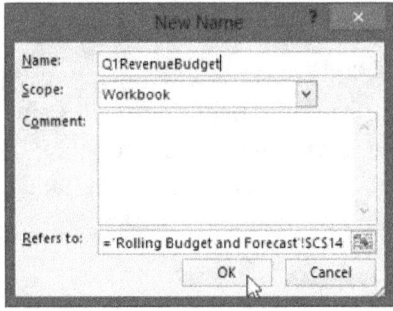

Step 5: Select a different scope for the reference, if desired, from the **Scope** drop down list.

Step 6: Enter a **Comment**, if desired,

Step 7: Change the **Refers to** area, if desired.

Step 8: Select **OK**.

To use a named range in a formula, use the following procedure.

Step 1: Begin entering your formula.

Step 2: When you are ready to enter the range, select the **Formula** tab.

Step 3: Select **Use in Formula**.

Step 4: Select the named range from the list.

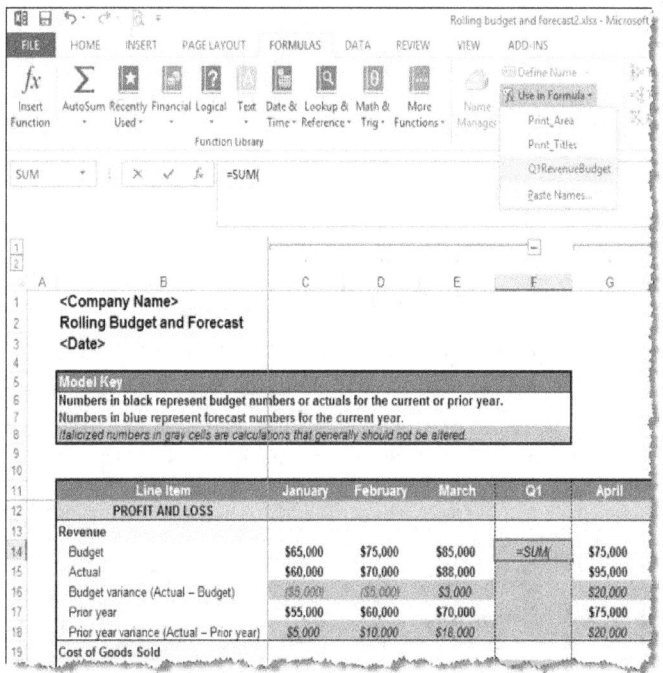

Understanding Formula Errors

Discuss the most common formula errors and how they occur.

Start every function with the equal sign (=)

Excel will display the formula contents as text or a date if you do not use the equal sign.

Match all open and close parentheses

Every parenthesis needs a pair. Parenthesis must be in the correct position for the formula to work correctly.

Use a colon to indicate a range

When working with a range of cells, you must use a colon between the first and last cell reference.

Enter all required arguments

Some functions require arguments and some do not. If the function requires arguments, make sure you have the right number.

Enter the correct type of arguments

For functions that require arguments, make sure you have the right ones.

Use the * symbol when multiplying numbers

The * symbol (asterisk) is the multiplication operator in Excel, not "x."

Use quotation marks around text in formulas

If you create a formula that includes text, enclose the text in quotation marks.

Nest no more than 64 functions

The top limit of nested functions, or functions within a function, is 64.

Enclose other sheet names in single quotation marks

If your worksheet names contain non-alphabetical characters, you must enclose the sheet name within single quotation marks when using the name in a formula.

Place an exclamation point (!) after a worksheet name when you refer to it in a formula

If you are using a worksheet name in a formula, the name must be followed by an exclamation point.

Include the path to external workbooks

If you are referencing cells from another workbook, make sure the formula includes both the workbook name and the path to the workbook.

Enter numbers without formatting

Excel treats commas as separator characters. Format the formula result after you enter the numbers in the formula.

Avoid dividing by zero

If you divide a cell by another that is zero or no value can result in a #DIV/0! Error.

Using Error Checking

The *Error Checking* dialog box, use the following procedure.

Step 1: From anywhere on the worksheet, select the **Formulas** tab.

Step 2: Select **Error Checking**.

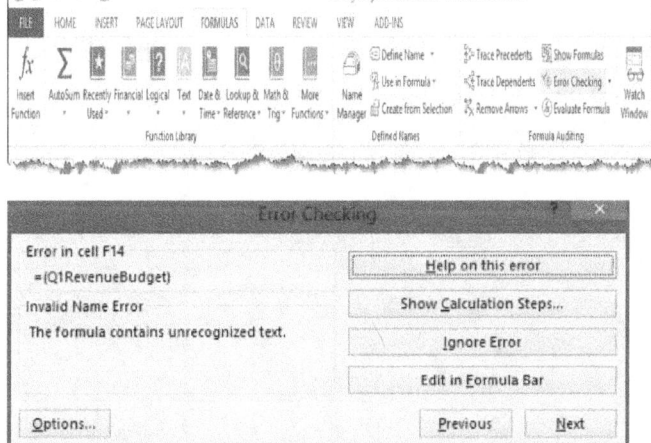

The Error Checking dialog box displays the formula as written in the cells. It explains why the formula contains an error.

- **Help on this Error** – opens the Excel help files directly to an article related to the type of error Excel detected.

- **Show Calculation steps** – opens the Evaluate Formula dialog box (discussed later in this chapter).

- **Ignore Error** – allows you to keep the error and removes the green triangle from the cell.

- **Edit in Formula Bar** – moves your cursor to the Formula bar to allow you to correct the formula.

- **Options** – opens the Options window to allow you to adjust the error checking options.

- **Resume** – restarts the Error Checking if you have switched to another task.

- **Previous** – returns to the previous error.

- **Next** – moves to the next error.

The Excel Options dialog box for Formulas.

You can open the Formulas options from the Error Checking dialog box or the Trace Errors commands next to an error cell.

You can also open the Options dialog box selecting the **File** tab from the Ribbon. Then select **Options**. Select **Formulas**.

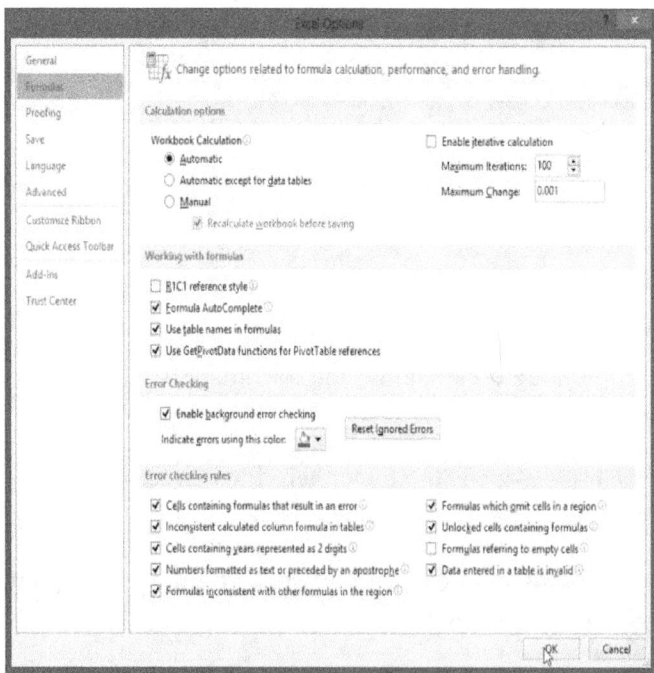

Under Error Checking, you can turn on **Background error checking** by checking the box.

You can change the color of the triangle displayed in cells where Excel has detected a formula error.

Select the **Reset Ignored Errors** to re-enable Excel to help you with any errors that you have previously ignored.

In the Error Checking Rules area, you can check or clear the following checkboxes:

- **Cells containing Formulas that result in an error** – When checked, Excel checks for formulas that do not use expected syntax, arguments, or data types.

- **Inconsistent calculated column formula in tables** – When checked, Excel checks for inconsistencies in calculated columns, such as when you enter data other than a formula in a column that has all calculated cells.

- **Cells containing years represented in 2 digits** – When checked, Excel will create an error if you enter a date with a year represented as two digits.

- **Numbers formatted in text or preceded by an apostrophe** – When checked, Excel will create an error if you enter or import numbers preceded by an apostrophe or text.

- **Formulas inconsistent with other formulas in the region** – When checked, Excel looks for formulas that are different from formulas near it. Often these formulas should be the same, except for the cell references used.

- **Formulas which omit cells in a region** – When checked, Excel compares the reference in a formula against the actual range of cells adjacent to it.

- **Unlocked cells containing formulas** – Formulas are locked for protection by default and must be unlocked before editing. If you have unlocked cells with formulas, Excel marks it as an error when this box is checked.

- **Formulas referring to empty cells** – When checked, Excel creates an error if a formula includes a reference to an empty cell.

- **Data entered in a table is invalid** – When checked, Excel creates an error if there is a validation error in a table.

Using the Trace Errors Commands

The Trace Errors Commands on a cell with a formula error, use the following procedure.

Step 1: A formula with an error displays a green triangle in the upper left corner, along with an error icon next to the cell. Click on the arrow next to the icon to see the options.

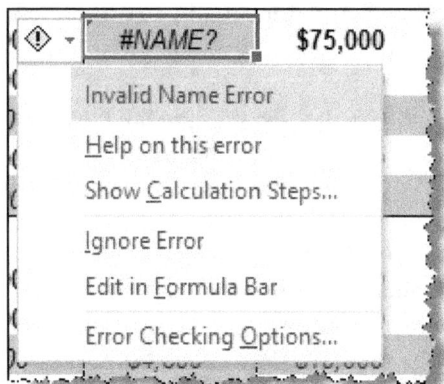

- **Help on this Error** – opens the Excel help files directly to an article related to the type of error Excel detected.

- **Show Calculation steps** – opens the Evaluate Formula dialog box (discussed later in this chapter).

- **Ignore Error** – allows you to keep the error and removes the error icon and green triangle.

- **Edit in Formula Bar** – moves your cursor to the Formula bar to allow you to correct the formula.

- **Error Checking Options** – opens the Options window to allow you to adjust the error checking options (discussed later in this chapter).

Evaluating Formulas

To evaluate a formula, use the following procedure.

Step 1: Select the cell that contains the formula you want to evaluate.

Step 2: Select the **Formulas** tab.

Step 3: Select **Evaluate Formula**.

Step 4: Select **Evaluate** to see the results of the underlined portion of the formula.

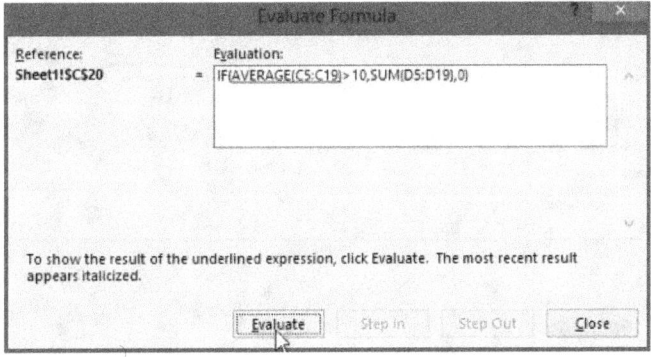

Step 5: Continue selecting **Evaluate** to see the results of each piece of the formula.

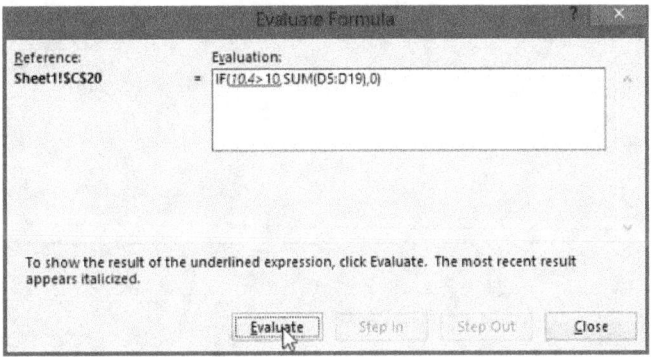

- If the underlined part of the formula is a reference to another formula, select **Step In** to display the other formula in the **Evaluation** box. Select **Step Out** to go back to the previous cell and formula. The **Step In** button is not available the second time a reference appears in the formula, or if the formula refers to a cell in a separate workbook.

- To see the evaluation again, click **Restart**.

Step 6: Select **Close** when you have finished.

Evaluate each of the formulas and discuss why the results are different, even though the same formula is used for each column of cells.

Chapter 9 – Using What If Analysis

"What-if" analysis allows you to have Excel change the values in cells so that you can see how those changes affect the formulas outcomes. There are three kinds of what if analysis: goal seek, scenarios, and data tables. Goal seek allows you to find the necessary value for an unknown in a formula to obtain desired results. Scenarios allow you to view multiple different possible results for up to 32 variables. Data tables allow you to quickly calculate multiple results for one or two variables in one operation. You can view and compare the results of all the different variations together on your worksheet. This chapter introduces these tools.

Using Goal Seek

To use goal seek, use the following procedure.

Step 1: When using goal seek, one value from a formula should be left blank.

Step 2: Select the **Data** tab from the Ribbon.

Step 3: Select **What If Analysis**.

Step 4: Select **Goal Seek**.

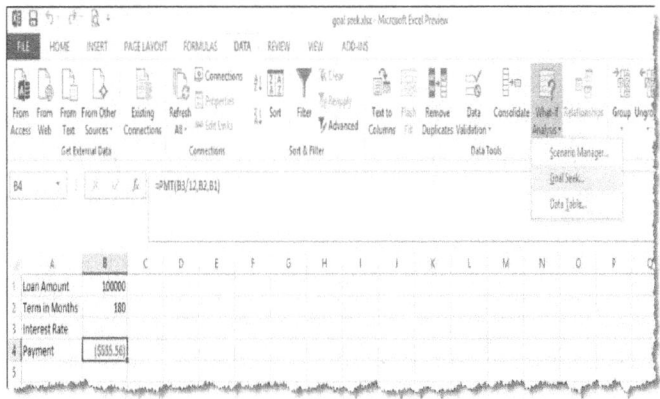

Excel displays the *Goal Seek* dialog box.

Step 1: In the **Set Cell** field, enter or select from the worksheet the cell that contains the formula. In the sample file, select B4.

Step 2: In the **To Value** field, enter the formula result you want. For example, in the sample file, you may want the resulting payment of $900. You would enter **-900** because it is a payment.

Step 3: In the **By Changing Cell** field, enter or select the reference for the cell that contains the value you do not know. In the sample file, this is B3.

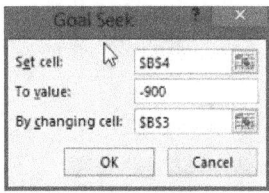

Step 4: Select **OK**.

Excel displays the *Goal Seek Status* dialog box. Select **OK** to close it.

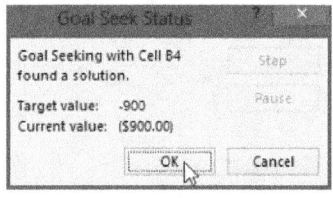

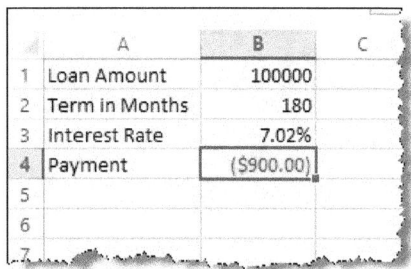

You may need to reformat the cell with the new answer to view the answer in the preferred format.

Using the Scenario Manager

To add a scenario, use the following procedure.

Step 1: Select the **Data** tab from the Ribbon.

Step 2: Select **What If Analysis**.

Step 3: Select **Scenario Manager**.

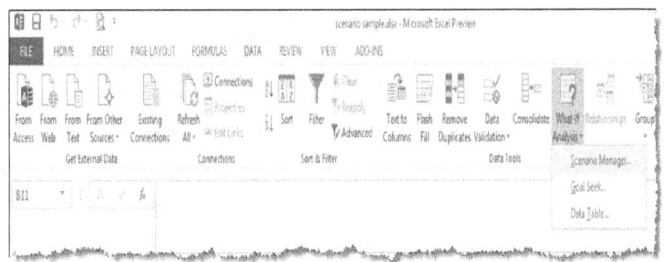

Step 4: In the *Scenario Manager* dialog box, select **Add** to create a new scenario.

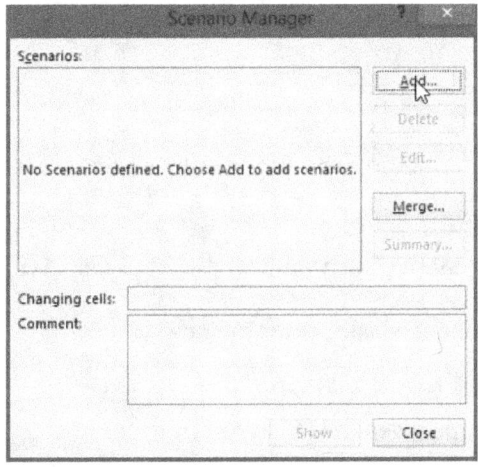

Step 5: In the *Add Scenario* dialog box, enter a **Scenario Name**.

Step 6: In the **Changing Cells** field, enter (or select from the worksheet) the multiple cells of changing values in the first scenario. Press the CTRL key while selecting each value.

Step 7: Enter a **Comment**, if desired.

Step 8: Protect the scenario by checking the **Prevent changes** and/or the **Hide** boxes.

Step 9: Select **OK**.

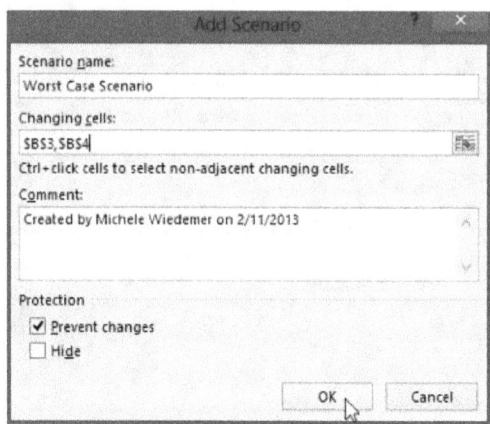

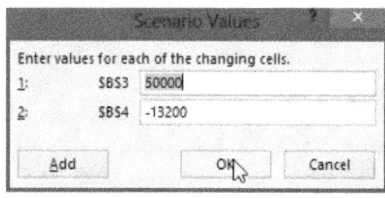

Step 10: The *Scenario values* dialog box shows the values you selected.

- For the original scenario, keep the values Excel displays.

- For each subsequent scenario, enter the new values.

Step 11: Select **Add** to create another set of values. If you have finished adding all the possibilities, select **OK** to return to the Scenario Manager.

Step 12: Repeat steps 4 through 10 to create another scenario.

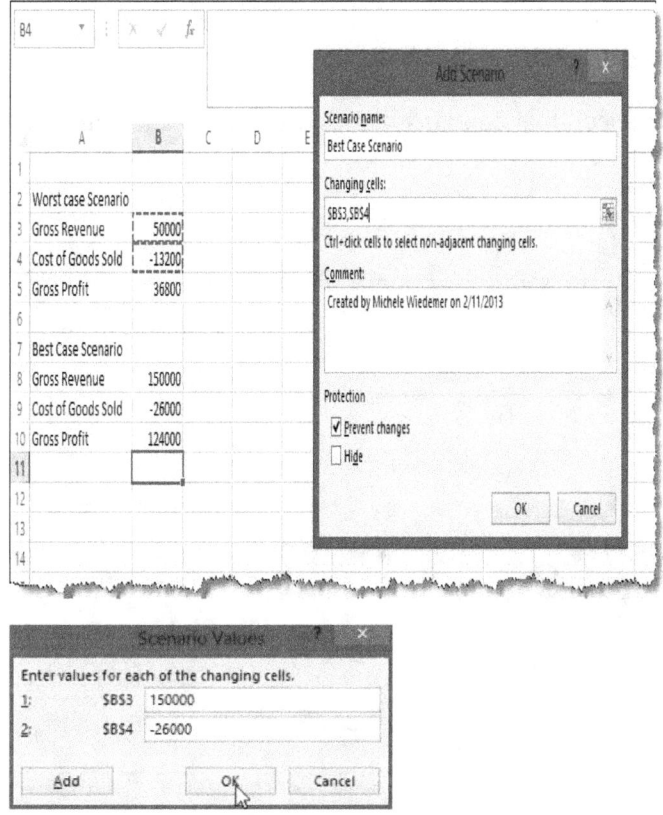

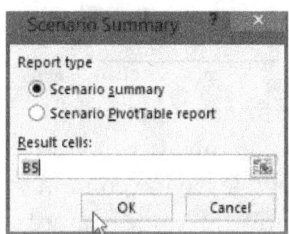

Step 13: On the *Scenario Manager* dialog box, you can select a scenario name and select **Show** to see the results. The contents of the cells change, depending on which scenario you select and show. To view a report, select **Summary.**

Excel displays the *Scenario Summary* dialog box.

Step 14: Indicate whether Excel should display the **Scenario Summary** or a **Scenario PivotTable Report**.

Step 15: Select the cell that contains the results you want to compare (or the formula cell).

Step 16: Select **OK**.

Excel displays your results in the selected format.

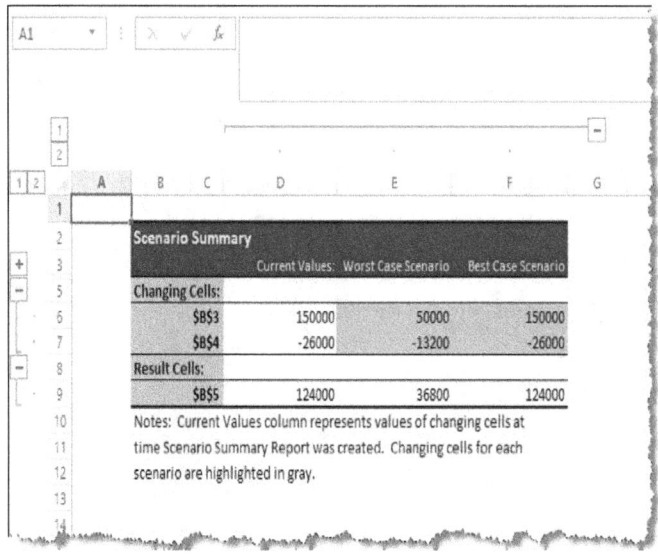

Using a One Input Data Table

To set up a one-input data table, use the following procedure.

Step 1: Enter the known values that the formula will use in evaluating the variable values.

Step 2: Enter the list of values you want to use for the input cell for the formula either down one column or across one row. If you are entering the values in a column, as shown below, leave the column to the right empty. Also leave additional rows below the values empty. If you are entering the values in a row, leave the rows below the values empty. Also leave a few columns to the right empty.

	A	B	C	D
1	Mortgage Loan Analysis			Payments
2	Down Payment	None		
3	Interest Rate		9.00%	
4	Term(months)	360	9.25%	
5	Loan Amount	80000	9.50%	
6				
7				
8				
9				

Step 3: If you have entered your data in columns, enter the formula one cell above and one cell to the right of the list of data values. You can enter additional formulas in the cells to the right of this cell to evaluate how the data values affect other formulas. If you have entered your data in rows, enter the formula one column to the left of the first value and one cell below the row of values.

D2	▼	:	✗ ✓ fx	=PMT(B3/12,B4,-B5)

	A	B	C	D	E
1	Mortgage Loan Analysis			Payments	
2	Down Payment	None		=PMT(B3/12,B4,-B5)	
3	Interest Rate		9.00%		
4	Term(months)	360	9.25%		
5	Loan Amount	80000	9.50%		
6					
7					
8					

Step 4: Select the data table values and the formula. In this example, the range is C2:D5.

Step 5: Select the **Data** tab from the Ribbon.

Step 6: Select **What If Analysis**.

Step 7: Select **Data Table**.

Step 8: Select the input cell in the formula. In a one-input data table, you will only have one input. In this example, the cell B3 is the **Column Input** cell.

Step 9: Select **OK**.

For each possible value for the variable listed in the data table, Excel displays the results.

	A	B	C	D	E
1	Mortgage Loan Analysis			Payments	
2	Down Payment	None		$222.22	
3	Interest Rate		9.00%	643.6980936	
4	Term(months)	360	9.25%	658.1403404	
5	Loan Amount	80000	9.50%	672.6833657	
6					
7					

You may want to format the cells to show the results with the desired formatting (such as currency in this example).

Using a Two Input Data Table

To set up a two input data table, use the following procedure.

Step 1: Enter the known values that the formula will use in evaluating the variable values. In this example, using the previous lesson's workbook, delete the numbers except for the Loan Amount.

Step 2: Enter the formula. In this example, it should be entered in cell C2.

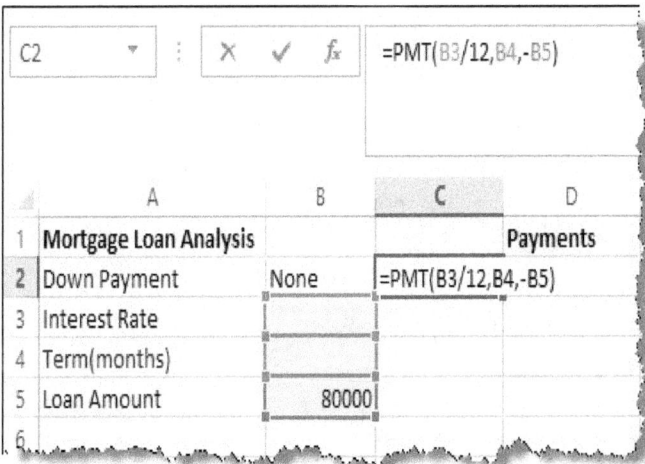

C2	▾	⋮	✕	✓	f_x	=PMT(B3/12,B4,-B5)

	A	B	C	D
1	Mortgage Loan Analysis			Payments
2	Down Payment	None	=PMT(B3/12,B4,-B5)	
3	Interest Rate			
4	Term(months)			
5	Loan Amount	80000		
6				

Step 3: Enter the list of values for the first input cell for the formula down one column under the formula. In this example, the unknown interest rate is the first input cell.

	A	B	C	D	E
1	Mortgage Loan Analysis			Payments	
2	Down Payment	None	#NUM!		
3	Interest Rate		9.00%		
4	Term(months)		9.25%		
5	Loan Amount	80000	9.50%		
6					
7					

Step 4: Enter the list of values for the second input cell for the formula across in one row next to the formula. In this example, the unknown term is the second input cell.

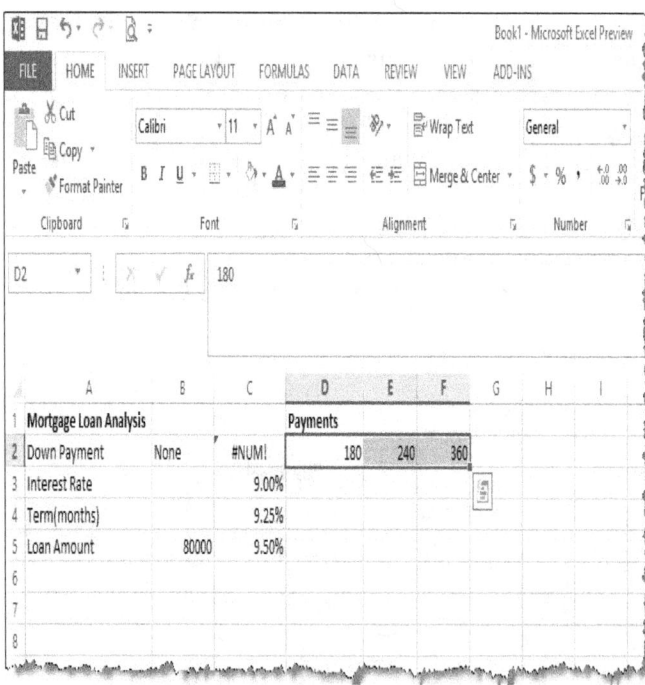

Step 5: Select the range that includes data table values, the formula, and the area where Excel will display the results. In this example, the range is C2:D5.

Step 6: Select the **Data** tab from the Ribbon.

Step 7: Select **What If Analysis**.

Step 8: Select **Data Table**.

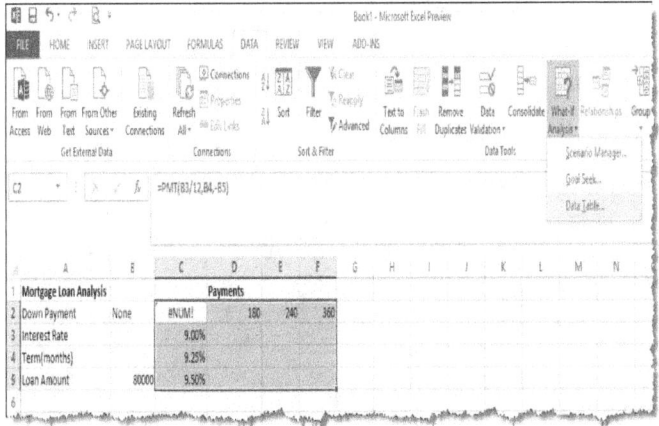

Step 9: Select the **Row input cell** in the formula. In this example, the cell B4 is the Row Input cell.

Step 10: Select the Column input cell in the formula. In this example, the cell B3 is the Column Input cell.

Step 11: Select **OK**.

For each possible value for the variable listed in the data table, Excel displays the results.

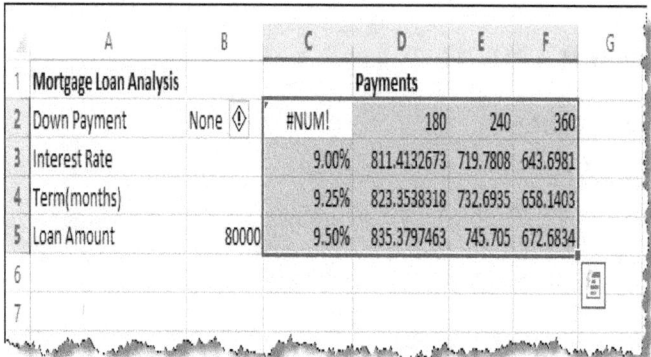

	A	B	C	D	E	F	G
1	Mortgage Loan Analysis			Payments			
2	Down Payment	None ◈	#NUM!	180	240	360	
3	Interest Rate		9.00%	811.4132673	719.7808	643.6981	
4	Term(months)		9.25%	823.3538318	732.6935	658.1403	
5	Loan Amount	80000	9.50%	835.3797463	745.705	672.6834	
6							
7							

You may want to format the cells to show the results with the desired formatting (such as currency in this example).

Chapter 10 – Managing Your Data

In this chapter, you will learn how to transpose data from rows to columns. You will also learn about the Text to Columns feature. This chapter explains how to check for duplicates and create data validation rules. You will also learn how to consolidate data.

Transposing Data from Rows to Columns

To transpose data, use the following procedure.

Step 1: Copy the range of cells you want to transpose. This feature will not work if you cut the cells.

Step 2: Place your cursor in the new location and right-click.

Step 3: Select **Transpose** from the **Paste Options** on the context menu.

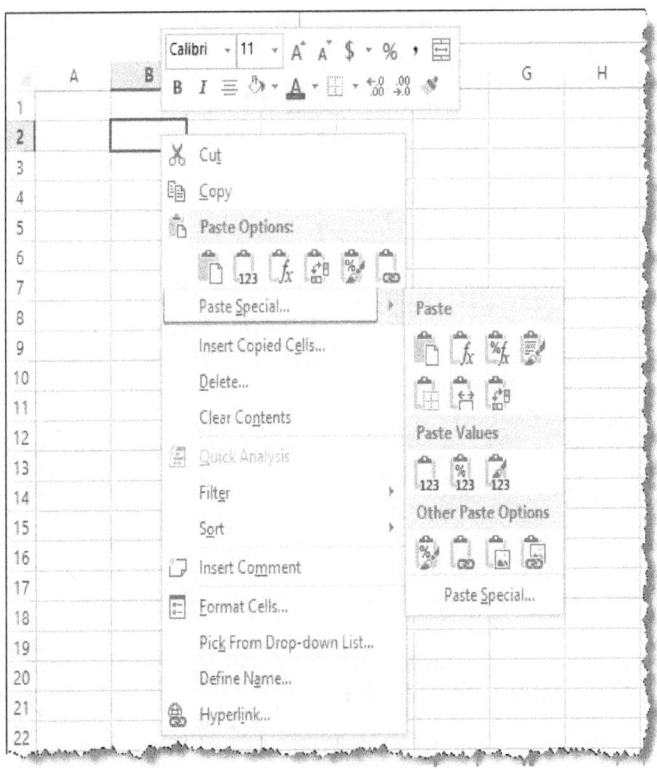

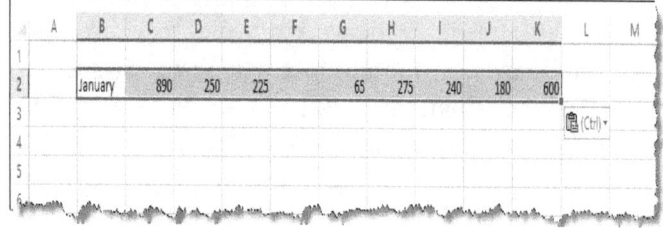

Using the Text to Columns Feature

To convert text to columns, use the following procedure.

Step 1: Paste text from another application.

Step 2: Select the text.

Step 3: Select the **Data** tab from the Ribbon.

Step 4: Select **Text to Columns**.

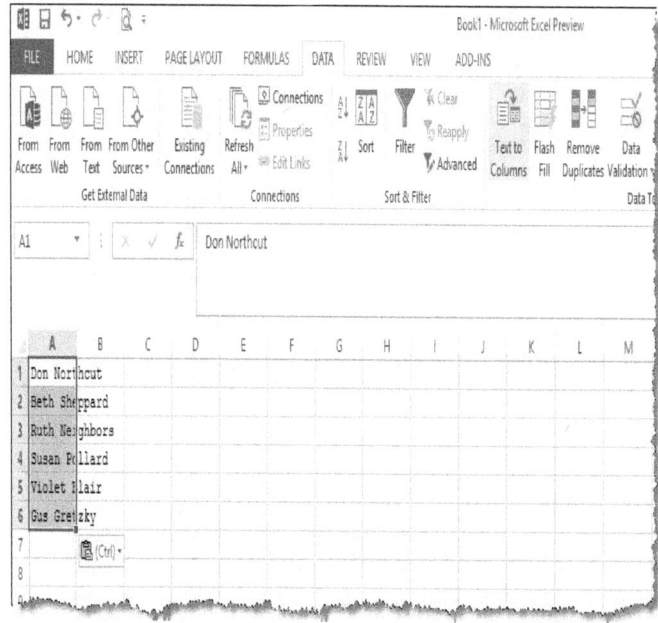

Step 5: In the *Convert Text to Columns Wizard*, choose the file type that best describes your data. Select **Next**.

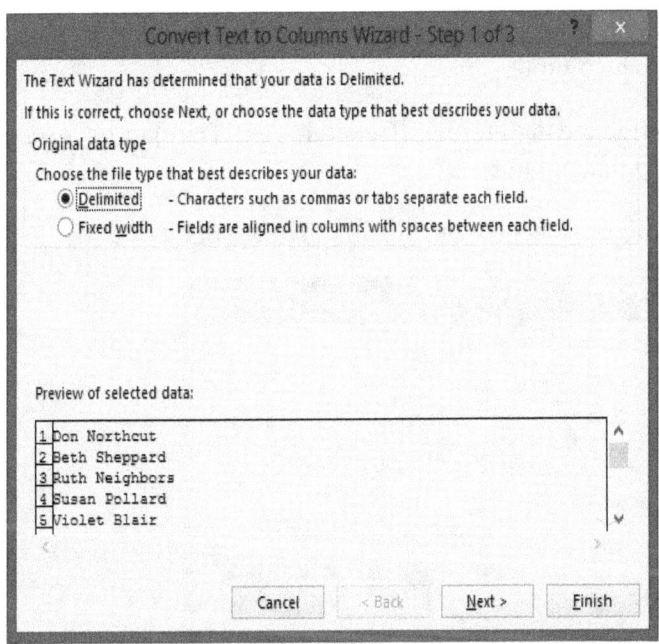

Step 6: In the next screen, select the type of divider. In this example, a space separates the items we want to convert to columns. Your text could be divided by almost any character. Select **Next**.

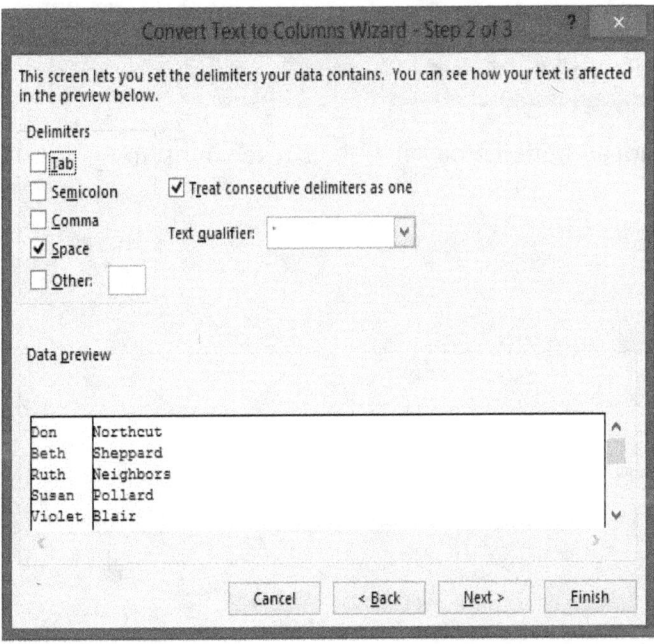

Step 7: In the next screen, you see a preview of the data converted to columns. For each column:

- Define the data format (General, Text, Date) or choose to skip that column.

- Enter or select the destination on the worksheet.

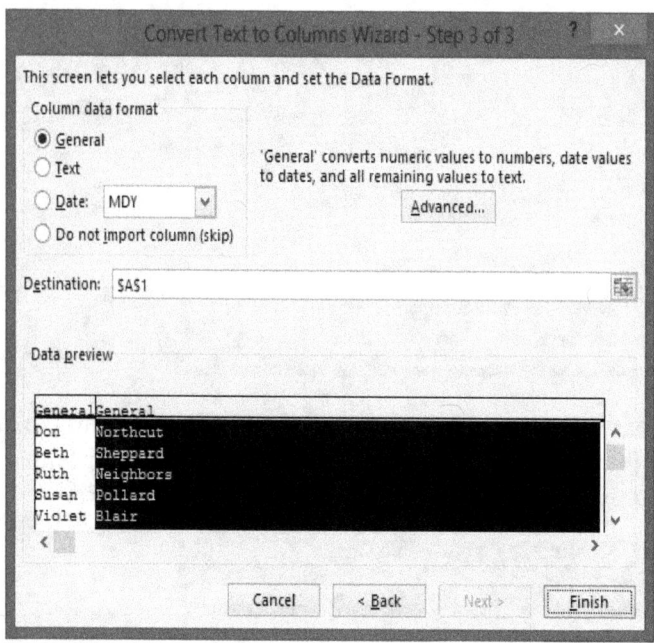

Using the **Advanced** button, you can also choose your settings for numeric data.

Advanced Text Import Settings

Settings used to recognize numeric data

Decimal separator: `.`

Thousands separator: `,`

Note: Numbers will be displayed using the numeric settings specified in the Regional Settings control panel.

Reset ☑ Trailing minus for negative numbers

OK   Cancel

Step 8: When you have finished, select **Finish**.

You can now work with your data as separate columns.

Checking for Duplicates

To check for duplicate data, use the following procedure.

Step 1: Highlight the area from which you want to remove duplicates.

Step 2: Select the **Data** tab from the Ribbon.

Step 3: Select **Remove Duplicates**.

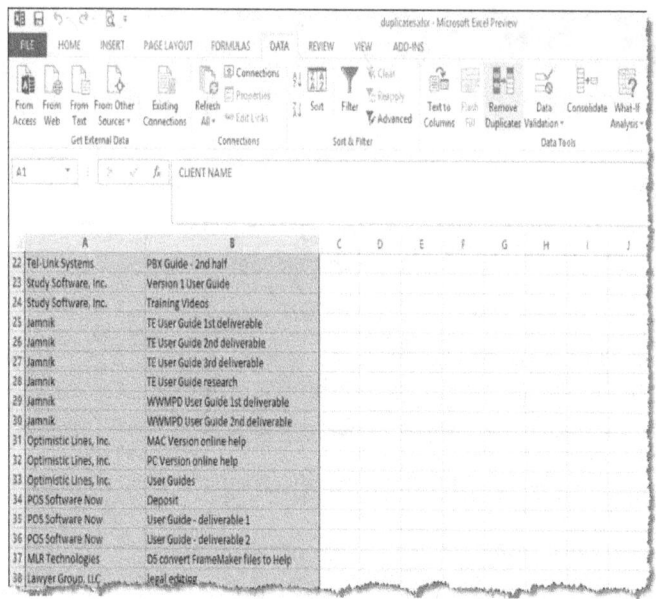

Step 4: Select the columns you want to check for duplicates. The **Select All** and **Unselect All** tools can help you manage a large list of columns. The **My Data has Headers** box indicates whether the list includes header rows.

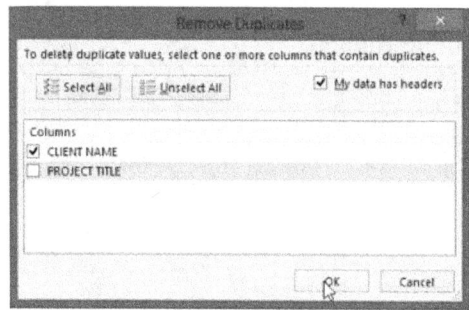

Step 5: Select **OK**.

Excel notifies you of how many duplicates are removed.

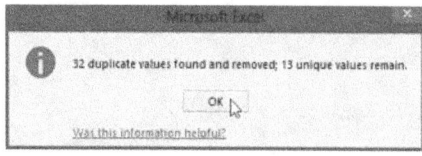

Creating Data Validation Rules

To create a data validation rule, use the following procedure.

Step 1: Select the cells where you want to apply the data validation rule.

Step 2: Select the **Data** tab from the Ribbon.

Step 3: Select **Data Validation**.

Step 4: Select **Data Validation** from the drop down list.

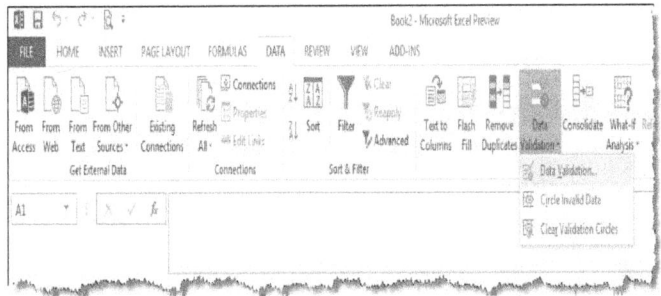

Step 5: On the **Settings** tab of the *Data Validation* dialog box, set up the **Validation Criteria**. Use the drop down lists to help you build your criteria. In this example, we are requiring a three-digit number.

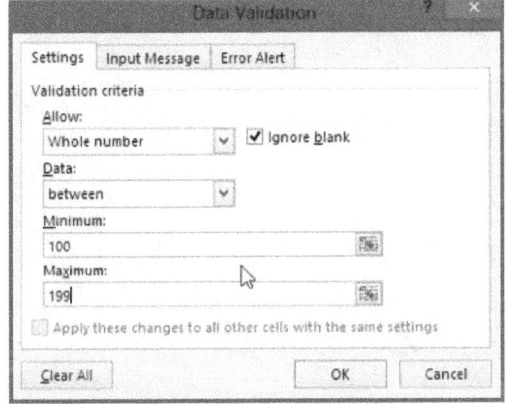

Step 6: Select the **Input Message** tab.

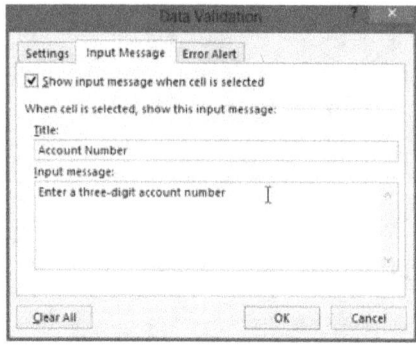

Step 7: Enter a **Title** and **Message** that the user will see when he or she selects the cell.

Step 8: Select the **Error Alert** tab.

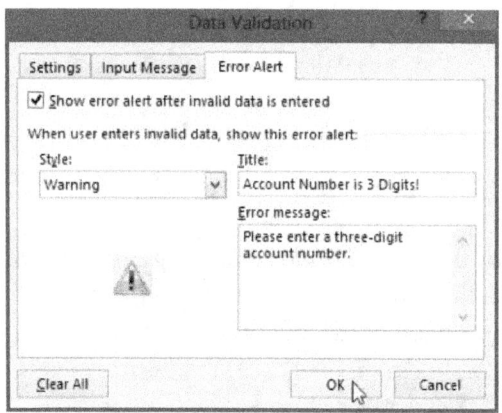

Step 9: Select the **Style** of error from the drop down list. Enter a **Title** and **Error** message to display if the user enters invalid data.

Step 10: Select **OK**.

Review what happens when you break the validation rule.

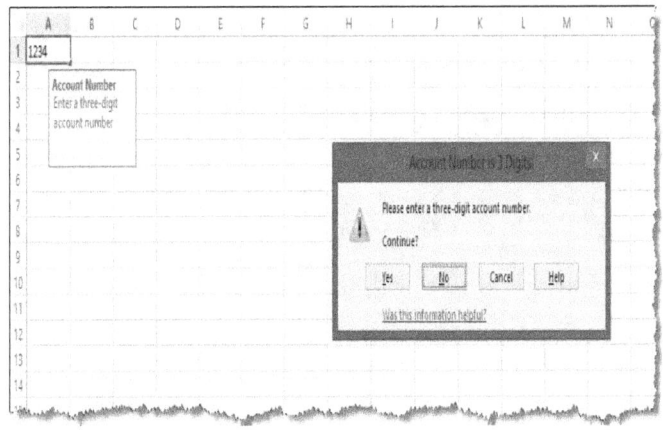

Consolidating Data

To consolidate data, use the following procedure.

Step 1: Select the starting cell where you want to display the consolidated data. Make sure to leave enough room for the consolidated data, so that you do not overwrite other information. In this example, choose the top left cell in Sheet 3.

Step 2: Select the **Data** tab from the Ribbon.

Step 3: Select **Consolidate**.

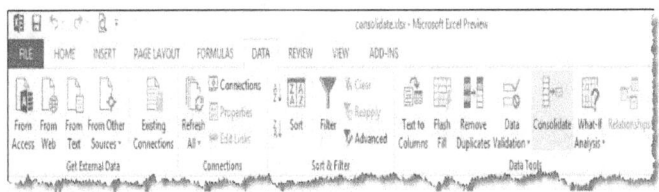

Step 4: In the *Consolidate* dialog box, do the following:

- Select the **Function** from the drop down list. In this example, use **Average**.

- Select the **Reference** for each worksheet you are consolidating. If the worksheet is in another workbook, select **Browse** to open it. Select the cells to include in the consolidation from the first worksheet and select **Add**. Repeat for each reference.

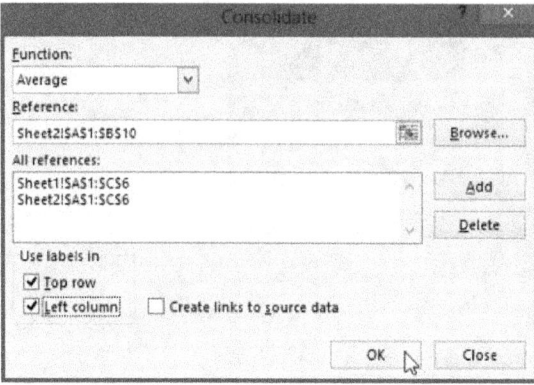

Chapter 11 – Grouping and Outlining Data

Excel has some powerful tools to help you quickly group and outline your data. In this chapter, you will learn how to group your data. You will also learn about adding subtotals to a list of data. This chapter explains outlining data. It also explains how to view grouped and outlined data.

Grouping Data

To create a group, use the following procedure.

Step 1: Select the range of cells you want to group.

Step 2: Select the **Data** tab from the Ribbon.

Step 3: Select **Group**.

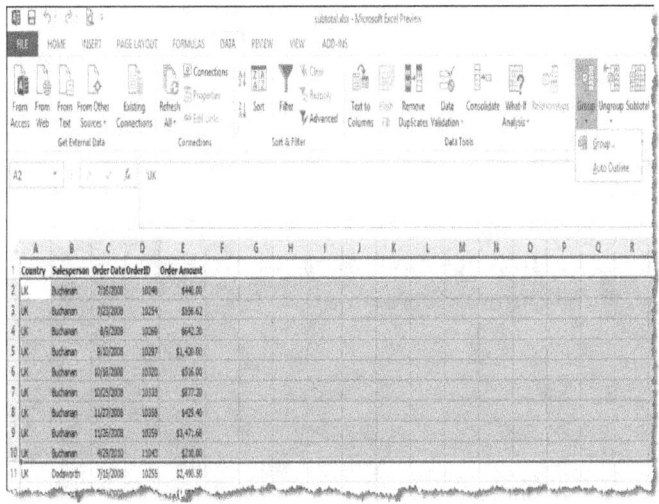

Adding Subtotals

To add subtotals, use the following procedure.

Step 1: Make sure that each column of data has a label in the first row. It must also contain similar facts. Do not include any blank rows or columns.

Step 2: Select the **Data** tab from the Ribbon.

Step 3: Select **Subtotal**.

Step 4: In the *Subtotal* dialog box, select the locations for the subtotals from the **At each change in** drop down list.

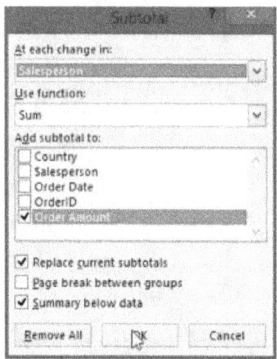

Step 5: Select the function to use in the subtotal fields from the **Use Function** drop down list.

Step 6: Check the boxes that correspond to your column headers for which column(s) to subtotal.

Step 7: Check the boxes to indicate the other formatting options by checking or clearing the **Replace current subtotals**, **Page break between groups**, and **Summary below data**.

Step 8: Select **OK**.

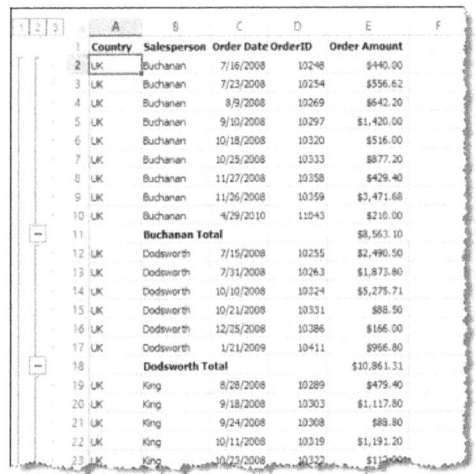

	A	B	C	D	E	F
1	Country	Salesperson	Order Date	OrderID	Order Amount	
2	UK	Buchanan	7/16/2008	10248	$440.00	
3	UK	Buchanan	7/23/2008	10254	$556.62	
4	UK	Buchanan	8/9/2008	10269	$642.20	
5	UK	Buchanan	9/10/2008	10297	$1,420.00	
6	UK	Buchanan	10/18/2008	10320	$516.00	
7	UK	Buchanan	10/25/2008	10333	$877.20	
8	UK	Buchanan	11/27/2008	10358	$429.40	
9	UK	Buchanan	11/26/2008	10359	$3,471.68	
10	UK	Buchanan	4/29/2010	11043	$210.00	
11		Buchanan Total			$8,563.10	
12	UK	Dodsworth	7/15/2008	10255	$2,490.50	
13	UK	Dodsworth	7/31/2008	10263	$1,873.80	
14	UK	Dodsworth	10/10/2008	10324	$5,275.71	
15	UK	Dodsworth	10/21/2008	10331	$88.50	
16	UK	Dodsworth	12/25/2008	10386	$166.00	
17	UK	Dodsworth	1/21/2009	10411	$956.80	
18		Dodsworth Total			$10,861.31	
19	UK	King	8/28/2008	10289	$479.40	
20	UK	King	9/18/2008	10303	$1,117.80	
21	UK	King	9/24/2008	10308	$88.80	
22	UK	King	10/11/2008	10319	$1,191.20	
23	UK	King	10/23/2008	10332	$1,172.00	

Outlining Data

To create an outline, use the following procedure.

Step 1: Select the range of cells to include in the outline.

Step 2: Select the **Data** tab from the Ribbon.

Step 3: Select the small square in the corner of the **Outline** group.

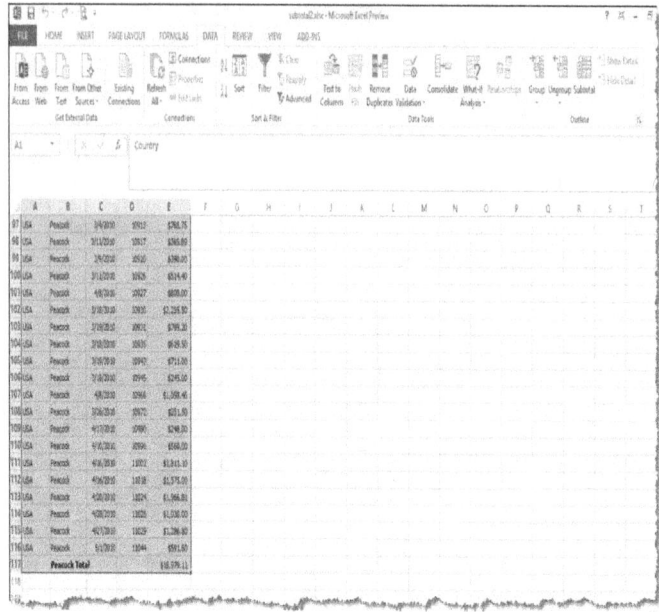

Step 4: In the *Settings* dialog box, check the direction of the summary rows and columns.

Step 5: Check the **Automatic styles** box to have Excel automatically apply styles to the outline.

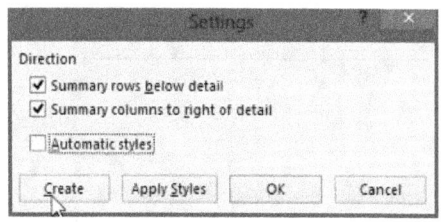

Step 6: Select **Create**.

Viewing Grouped and Outlined Data

To work with grouped or outlined data.

The **Hide Detail** icon allows you to quickly hide the detail data.

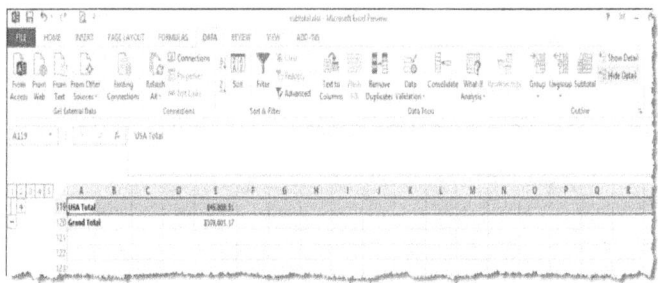

The + icons indicate hiding detail data.

The **Show Detail** icon allows you to quickly show the detail data. You can select the Show Detail icon multiple times to continue expanding the current level.

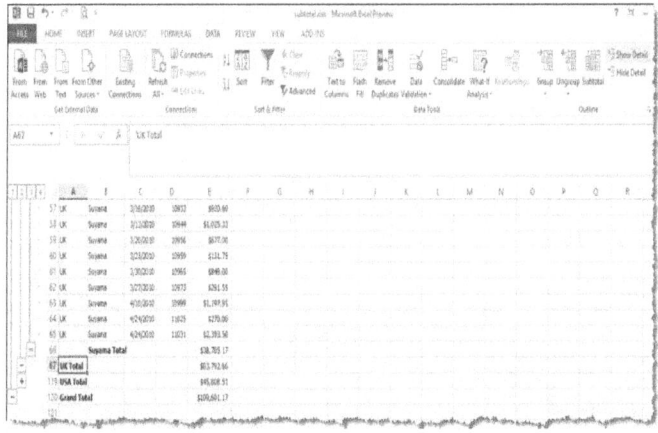

The minus icons allow you to collapse individual groups. The plus icons allow you to expand individual groups.

The numbers in the top left corner indicate a level. Click on a number to show that level.

			A	B	C	D	E	F
		1	Country	Salesperson	Order Date	OrderID	Order Amount	
	+	11		Buchanan Total			$8,563.10	
	+	18		Dodsworth Total			$10,861.31	
	+	27		King Total			$5,663.08	
	+	66		Suyama Total			$38,705.17	
−		67	UK Total				$63,792.66	
	+	74		Callahan Total			$6,961.00	
	+	87		Fuller Total			$15,020.50	
	+	95		Leverling Total			$4,847.90	
	+	118		Peacock Total			$18,979.11	
−		119	USA Total				$45,808.51	
−		120	Grand Total				$109,601.17	
		121						
		122						

Chapter 12 – Final Tips

We would like to leave you with a few thoughts to accompany you on your Excel learning journey.

- Use SmartArt, pictures, text boxes and shapes to enhance your workbooks. Remember that many objects have contextual tool tabs that appear when you select an object.

- Use precedent and dependent tracing to help you audit complicated formula dependencies.

- Excel recommends the charts that make the most sense for your selected data. Use the recommendations to save lots of time in creating charts. Remember that you can customize which elements appear on the chart, the style and color, and even apply filters.

- Add data labels to your chart to help explain the data.

- PivotTables and PivotCharts are interactive to help you summarize, analyze, explore and present your data. Feel free to experiment and watch the results.

- Use macros to automate repetitive tasks.

- Solve formula errors before they happen by using named ranges instead of cell references. This explains to anyone viewing the worksheet more about the purpose of a formula. Remember that there are several tools to help you solve formula errors if they do occur.

- Use What If Analysis to see results of different variables in the same formula.

- Use outlining and groups to quickly managed summary and detail data.

- Practice as much as you can, and as soon as you can.

Additional Titles

The Technical Skill Builder series of books covers a variety of technical application skills. For the availability of titles please see https://www.silvercitypublications.com/shop/. Note the Master Class volume contains the Essentials, Advanced, and Expert (when available) editions.

Current Titles

Microsoft Excel 2013 Essentials

Microsoft Excel 2013 Advanced

Microsoft Excel 2013 Expert

Microsoft Excel 2013 Master Class

Microsoft Word 2013 Essentials

Microsoft Word 2013 Advanced

Microsoft Word 2013 Expert

Microsoft Word 2013 Master Class

Microsoft Project 2010 Essentials

Microsoft Project 2010 Advanced

Microsoft Project 2010 Expert

Microsoft Project 2010 Master Class

Microsoft Visio 2010 Essentials

Microsoft Visio 2010 Advanced

Microsoft Visio 2010 Master Class

Coming Soon

Microsoft Access 2013 Essentials

Microsoft Access 2013 Advanced

Microsoft Access 2013 Expert

Microsoft Access 2013 Master Class

Microsoft PowerPoint 2013 Essentials

Microsoft PowerPoint 2013 Advanced

Microsoft PowerPoint 2013 Expert

Microsoft PowerPoint 2013 Master Class

Microsoft Outlook 2013 Essentials

Microsoft Outlook 2013 Advanced

Microsoft Outlook 2013 Expert

Microsoft Outlook 2013 Master Class

Microsoft Publisher 2013 Essentials

Microsoft Publisher 2013 Advanced

Microsoft Publisher 2013 Master Class

Windows 7 Essentials

Windows 8 Essentials

www.ingramcontent.com/pod-product-compliance
Lightning Source LLC
LaVergne TN
LVHW051744050326
832903LV00029B/2707